21543

FIRE OF LOVE

In Memory of
Joseph Benedict Hunt
June 27, 1962
Feb. 18, 1964

FIRE OF LOVE

An anthology of Abbot Marmion's published writings on
the Holy Spirit

by

FATHER CHARLES DOLLEN

SANDS & Co (Publishers) LTD
15 King Street, London, W.C.2
76 Cambridge Street, Glasgow

Nihil obstat: JOANNES M. T. BARTON, S.T.D., L.S.S.
Censor deputatus

Imprimatur: PATRITIUS CASEY
Vic. Gen.

Westmonasterii, die 2 Julii, 1964

PRINTED IN GREAT BRITAIN BY
NORTHUMBERLAND PRESS LIMITED
GATESHEAD ON TYNE

Contents

		PAGE
Introduction: Flame of Love		7
1.	The Holy Spirit, the Spirit of Christ	11
2.	The Most Holy Trinity	13
3.	The distinction of Persons	17
4.	The Holy Spirit in the Trinity	19
5.	Holy, Holy, Holy!	23
6.	The Operations of the Holy Spirit in Christ	26
7.	The Holy Spirit and the Mysteries of Christ	31
8.	The Work of Pentecost Day	33
9.	The Holy Spirit in the Church	39
10.	The continuing Pentecost	42
11.	The Holy Spirit vivifies the Church	45
12.	The Sacrament of Divine Adoption	48
13.	The Indwelling Spirit	52
14.	The Gifts of the Holy Spirit	56
15.	The Gifts of Fear, of Piety and of Fortitude	61
16.	The Gifts of knowledge, understanding and counsel	63
17.	The Gift of wisdom	66
18.	The Holy Spirit and the Priest	69
19.	The Holy Spirit and the Liturgy	72
20.	The Holy Spirit and prayer	74

21. Preparation for prayer 79

22. Prayer and Grace 85

23. Union with God 89

24. Beginning the Spiritual Life 92

25. Progress in prayer 94

26. Growth in the Spirit 99

27. The life of prayer 101

28. Devotion to the Holy Spirit 105

29. Invoking the Holy Spirit 108

30. The Holy Spirit and Marmion 111

31. Our Lady of the Holy Spirit 113

Bibliography 121

Index 123

Introduction: Flame of Love

THE Holy Spirit, the divine flame of the personal, burning Love of the Father and the Son, descended in the sound of a mighty wind on the first Pentecost.[1] The tongues as of fire that distributed themselves from this divine flame started the conflagration of a divine romance on the birthday of the Church.

The apostles gave voice to this magnificent outpouring of Love and carried the sound of that Pentecostal wind to the ends of the earth. So vehement, so all-embracing was this advent of the Spirit of Jesus that the entire mystical body, from its birth to its final completion, was set on fire with the sparks from this flame.

Pope John XXIII was keenly aware of this truth when he sounded the call for a New Pentecost. He intended to direct our attention to, and our co-operation with, this Holy Spirit who resides always in the Church, ever refreshing, renewing, and re-forming it.[2]

The mission of the Holy Spirit to the Church is to form it into the perfect Body of Christ, fully in tune with each age of civilization, fully able to carry Christ effectively into the world of its time. The work of Divine Love is to inspire the Church to take the eternal truths that Christ taught into the changing market-place of the day and to make them meaningful in the common tongue.

The mission of the Holy Spirit to the individual Christian soul is to form Christ perfectly in each man, to teach him to think with Christ, live for Christ, and fill his heart with the sentiments of Christ. The work of this divine flame of Love is to make each Christian glow with the fire of divine love, to make his words and example effective with His divine unction, and to form each man into an effective unit in the mystical body.[3]

Abbot Columba Marmion was also keenly aware of this truth. The very fact that Marmion's spirituality is so completely and thoroughly Christ-centred made him turn directly to the Holy Spirit whose proper operation in us is the formation of the Christ-life.

[1] Acts 2:1-13. [2] John 16:6-16; also, John 14:16-26.
[3] Ephesians 5:29-30; 1 Cor. 6:15, etc.

7

Dom Marmion founded his entire school of ascetical and mystical theology on the fact of our predestination in Christ, our incorporation in Christ as sons and coheirs, by the grace of adoption.[4] He understood Christ to be the exemplary cause of all perfection, the satisfactory and meritorious cause, and, indeed, the efficient cause of our sanctification. Marmion recognized the mystery of the Church as inseparable from the mystery of Christ, that in His mystical body we are all one, in charity.[5]

But then, Abbot Marmion delved deeply "into those things" at which "angels desire to look."[6] What did he uncover? "We shall only perfectly grasp the mystery of Christ and the economy of our salvation, if we fix our attention upon this Divine Spirit and His action within us.[7]

He found, further, "The Holy Spirit is the agent of all sanctification in the Church. The supernatural activity of the children of God in its different degrees depends on His vivifying influence."[8] Thus, the very Christocentric orientation of Marmion's thought demanded that he turn himself to the Spirit of Jesus.

On March 3rd, 1900, he wrote of his own spiritual life, "I have a great desire to be guided, led, moved by the Spirit of Jesus in all things." And again, "I shall try to live in this Holy Spirit." No one can doubt, after studying the books of Abbot Marmion, that the action of the Holy Spirit was exceedingly fruitful in him.[9]

In this present volume, the works of Dom Marmion have been mined to seek out the thinking of this great Benedictine abbot on the Holy Spirit. It has been a tremendous experience just gathering this material and preparing it for publication. It is offered with the hope that it might introduce some souls into the New Pentecost so ardently desired by the late beloved Pope John.

In simple gratitude, I must acknowledge the Rev. Dr. Elmer McNamara, of St. Bernard's Seminary, Rochester, N.Y., who introduced me and a whole generation of priests to the theology of Abbot Marmion. Then, it was my privilege to learn, by word and example,

---

[4] Ephesians 1:4-6; Galatians 4:4-7.
[5] Christ the Life of the Soul, chapter V, intro.
[6] 1 Peter 1:12.
[7] Christ the Life of the Soul, Chapter XVI, introduction.
[8] Christ the ideal of the Priest, chapter XVI, section 1.
[9] Christ the ideal of the Priest, appendix, section 16.

from the late Abbot Albert Beston and the present Abbot Philip
O'Connor, of New Melleray Abbey, Dubuque, Iowa, that the appli-
cation of Dom Marmion's principles are valid in every walk of life. I
was fortunate enough to sit at the feet of my Bishop, the Most Rever-
end Charles Francis Buddy, during the more than four years that he
conducted his famous Dogma Seminar, and to marvel at his great
devotion to the Holy Spirit, a devotion that has obviously borne
great fruit. And finally, my years as chaplain to the Sisters of Social
Service in San Diego, who are dedicated by profession to the Holy
Spirit, have convinced me beyond words, of the efficacy of this
magnificent devotion. May their souls ever glow with " tongues as of
fire " from this Divine Flame of Love.

1. The Holy Spirit, the Spirit of Christ

AMONG the books of the Sacred Scriptures, we have under the title of the " Acts of the Apostles " the history of the first days of the Church. This account, due to the pen of St. Luke, who witnessed many of the facts he relates, is full of charm and life. We see in it how the Church, founded by Jesus upon the Apostles, developed in Jerusalem, and then extended gradually beyond Judea, chiefly owing to the preaching of St. Paul. The greater part of this book records the missions, labours and struggles of the great Apostle. We are able to follow him in nearly every stage of his evangelical career. These pages taken from life reveal to us what incessant tribulations St. Paul endured, what numberless difficulties he encountered, the adventures that befell him, the sufferings he bore during the many journeys he undertook for the spread of the name and glory of Jesus.

It is recounted in these " Acts " that when, in the course of his missions, St. Paul came to Ephesus, he met there with some disciples and asked them, " Have you received the Holy Spirit since you believed? " The disciples answered him, " We haven't even heard that there is a Holy Spirit."

We are certainly not ignorant of the existence of the Holy Spirit. Yet how many Christians there are nowadays who only know His name and hardly anything of His work in souls! However, the Divine economy cannot be perfectly conceived unless we have as clear an idea as possible of what the Holy Spirit is for us.

In almost every text where St. Paul exposes the eternal designs concerning our supernatural adoption, and whenever he speaks of grace or of the Church, he speaks at the same time of " the Spirit of God ", " the Spirit of Christ " or " the Spirit of Jesus ". " You have received a spirit of adoption as sons by virtue of which we cry ' Abba! Father ' "[1] " God has sent the Spirit of His Son into our hearts, crying ' Abba, Father,' " so in truth we may call God our Father.[2] " Do you not know," he says elsewhere, " that you are

Christ the Life of the Soul, chapter VI, introduction.
[1] Rom. 8:15.   [2] Gal. 4:6.

the temple of God and that the Spirit of God dwells in you? "³ And again, "Or do you not know that your members are the temple of the Holy Spirit who is in you? "⁴

It is in Christ that all the well ordered edifice is raised to form a holy temple in the Lord; it is in Him that we are to be made, through the Holy Spirit, a temple which God inhabits.⁵ So that, as we form but one body in Christ, so we are all animated by one Spirit.⁶ The presence of this Spirit in our souls is so necessary that St. Paul says, "If anyone does not have the Spirit of Christ, he does not belong to Christ."⁷

You now understand why the Apostle, who longed for nothing so much as to see Christ live in the souls of his disciples, asked them if they had received the Holy Spirit. It was because they only are God's children, in Jesus Christ, who are led by the spirit of God.

We shall only perfectly grasp the mystery of Christ and the economy of our sanctification, if we fix our attention upon this Divine Spirit and His action within us. We have seen that the aim of all our life is to enter with great humility into God's thoughts and to adapt ourselves to them as perfectly as possible with childlike simplicity.

These thoughts being divine, their efficacy is intrinsically absolute. They infallibly produce fruits of sanctification, if we accept them with faith and love. Now, to enter into the divine plan, we must not only receive Christ⁸, but, as St. Paul points out, we must also "receive the Holy Spirit" and be submissive to His actions so as to be "one with Christ."

Consider Our Lord Himself. In that wonderful discourse after the Last Supper, when He reveals to those He calls His "friends" the secrets of the Eternal life He brings to them, He speaks of the Holy Spirit almost as often as he does of His Father. He tells them that this Spirit will take His place among them when He shall have ascended into Heaven; that this Spirit will be for them the Master of their inner life, a Master so necessary that Jesus Himself prays to His Father that this Spirit may be given to them and may abide with them.

And why should our Divine Saviour have been so intent on speaking of the Holy Spirit at this solemn hour and have done so in such

---

³ 1 Cor. 3:16.   ⁴ 1 Cor. 6:19.   ⁵ Ephes. 2:21-22.
⁶ Ephes. 4:4.   ⁷ Rom. 8:9.   ⁸ John 1:12.

pressing words, if what He tells us was to remain for us as a dead letter? Would it not be to do Him a wrong and cause great detriment to ourselves, if we were to pass over in silence a mystery so vital to us?

In his encyclical on the Holy Spirit ("Divinum illud munus" May 9, 1897) Pope Leo XIII bitterly deplores that "Christians have only a very poor knowledge of the Holy Spirit. They often use His name in their spiritual exercises but their faith is encompassed with great darkness". The great Pontiff likewise energetically insists that "all preachers and those who have the care of souls, should consider it a duty to teach the people carefully and at length about the Holy Spirit". He wishes that all subtle controversy be avoided as well as any rash attempt to pry into the deep nature of the mystery, but it is also his wish, "that the many and great benefits the Divine Giver has brought and ever brings to our souls should be recalled and clearly shown forth; for error or ignorance concerning these great and fruitful mysteries ought totally to disappear."

I will therefore try to show you, as clearly as I can, what the Holy Spirit is in Himself in the Adorable Trinity, His action over the Sacred Humanity of Christ, and the ceaseless benefits He brings to the Church and to souls. We shall thus complete the exposition of the Divine economy considered in itself.

Without doubt this subject is a very deep one and we ought to treat of it only with profound reverence. But, since Our Lord has revealed it to us, our faith ought also to consider it with love and confidence. Let us humbly ask the Holy Spirit Himself to enlighten our souls with a ray of His divine light. He will assuredly hear our prayer.

2. The Most Holy Trinity

FAITH reveals to us this truly astonishing mystery: the power and act of fecundity is one of the divine perfections.

God is the plenitude of being, the shoreless ocean of all perfection and of all life. The images of which we often make use to depict Him, the ideas we apply to Him by analogy in speaking of what is

Christ in His mysteries, chapter III, sections 1 and 2.

best in creatures, are powerless to represent Him. We shall never rise to a conception that does not belie God's infinity by merely extending, even infinitely, the limits of created being. We must recognize, in the most positive manner, that there are no limits where God is concerned. He is very Being, the necessary Being, subsisting of Himself, and possessing the plenitude of perfection.

Revelation teaches us this marvel of God's fecundity. There is in Him an altogether spiritual and ineffable paternity. He is Father, the principle of all divine life in the Trinity.

Being infinite Intelligence, God perfectly comprehends Himself. In a single act, He sees all that He is, all that is in Him. He comprehends, as it were, in a single glance, the plenitude of His perfections, and, in one thought, in one word that exhausts all His knowledge. This thought conceived by the eternal intelligence, this utterance whereby God expresses Himself is the Word. Faith tells us that this Word is God. "And the Word was God"[1] because the Word has (or rather, He is) with God one and the same divine nature.

And because the Father communicates to the Word a nature not only like unto His own, but identical with it, Holy Scripture tells us that He begets the Word, and it calls the Word, *the Son*. The inspired books repeat the ineffable exclamation of God contemplating His Son and proclaiming the beatitude of His eternal Fatherhood: From the bosom of My Divinity, before the creation of the light, I communicated life to Thee.[2] "Thou are my beloved Son, in thee I am well pleased."[3] Because this Son is indeed perfect, He possesses with the Father all the divine perfections saving the property of "being Father." So perfect is He that He is the equal of His Father by the unity of nature.

A creature can only give to another creature a nature like his own, but God begets God and gives to Him His own nature. It is God's glory to beget the Infinite and to contemplate Himself in another Himself, Who is His equal. So equal is the Son to the Father that He is the only-begotten, for there is only one Divine nature and the Son exhausts the eternal fecundity; therefore He is one with His Father. "I and the Father are one."[4]

Finally this beloved Son, equal to the Father, although distinct

---

[1] John 1:1.　　　　　　　　　　[2] Psalm 109:3.
[3] Luke 3:22; Mark 1:11.　　　　　[4] John 10:30.

from Him, and like Him a divine Person, does not leave the Father.
The Word ever dwells in the infinite Intelligence that conceives
Him; the Son ever dwells in the bosom of the Father Who begets
Him. He dwells there by the unity of nature. He also dwells there by
the love which they mutually bear to one another. From this proceeds, as from one principle, the Holy Spirit, the substantial love of
the Father and the Son.

You see what is the mysterious order of the ineffable communication of the intimate life of God in the Trinity. The Father, the
plenitude of all life, begets a Son; from the Father and the Son, as
from one principle, proceeds the Spirit of Love. All three have the
same eternity, the same infinity of perfection, the same wisdom, the
same power, the same sanctity, because the Divine nature is one for
the three Persons.

But each Person possesses exclusive properties—" to be Father, to
be Son, to proceed from the Father and the Son "—which establishes
ineffable relations between them and distinguishes them from each
other. There is an order or origin without there being either priority
of time or superiority of hierarchy or relation of dependance.

Such is the language of revelation. We could not have attained to
a knowledge of these things unless they had been revealed for us,
but Jesus Christ has willed, for the exercise of our faith and the joy
of our souls to give us this knowledge.

" Wherefore plunge into those abysses? Why has Christ Jesus dis-
closed them to us? Why does He return to them so often? And, so
as not to forget the sublimity of the Christian doctrine, ought we
not to dwell on these truths? But we must do so in trembling. We
must do so in faith. We must, while listening to Jesus Christ and
His altogether divine words, believe that these words come from one
who is God; and we must believe at the same time that this God
from whom they come, comes Himself from God, and that He is
Son; and at every word that we hear Him speak, we must rise as
high as the source, contemplating the Father in the Son and the Son
in the Father."[5]

When in eternity, we shall contemplate God, we shall see that it
is essential to infinite life, that it is natural to the divine Being, to be
one in three Persons. The true God whom we must know so as to

---

[5] Bossuet, *Meditations upon the Gospel.* The Last Supper, 1st part, 86th day.

have eternal life,[6] is He of whom we adore the trinity of Persons in the unity of nature.

Come! let us adore this marvellous fellowship in the unity, this wonderful equality of perfection in the distinction of Persons. O God, Father of incommensurable majesty, I adore Thee. I adore Thy Son for He, like Thee, is worthy of all reverence, being Thy true and only-begotten Son, God like Thyself! O Father, O Son, I adore your common Spirit, Your eternal bond of love. Blessed Trinity, I adore Thee!

In this Most Holy Trinity, the love of the Son for the Father is infinite. If He proclaims that He holds all from His Father, He likewise refers all to Him with love, and from this movement of dilection which meets that of the Father, proceeds that Third Person whom revelation calls by a mysterious name: the Holy Spirit, who is the substantial love of the Father and of the Son.

Here below, the love of Jesus for His father shines out in an ineffable manner. All Christ's life, all His mysteries are summed up in those words which St. John relates, "I love the Father."[7] Our Lord gave His disciples the infallible criterion of love. "If you keep my commandments you will abide in my love" and He at once gives an example, "As I also have kept my Father's commandments, and abide in His love."[8]

Jesus has ever remained in the love of the Father because He has always done His will. St. Paul expressly declares that the first movement of the Word-made-flesh was a movement of love: "Behold I come to do they will, O God!"[9] In this first glance of His earthly existence, the soul of Jesus saw the whole succession of His mysteries, the humiliations, the fatigues, the sufferings of which they were formed; and, by an act of love, He accepted to fulfil all these things.

This movement of love towards His Father has never ceased. Our Lord could say, "I do always the things that are pleasing to Him."[10] He fulfills everything to the last iota; He accepts all that His Father requires of Him, even to the bitter chalice of His agony: "Yet not my will but thine be done."[11] Even to the ignominious death of the cross, "that the world may know that I love the Father, and that I do as the Father commanded me."[12] And when all is consummated,

[6] John 17:3.   [7] John 14:31.   [8] John 15:10.
[9] Hebrews 10:7.   [10] John 8:29.   [11] Luke 22:42.
[12] John 14:31.

the last beat of His heart and His last thought are for the Father:
" Father, into Thy hands I commend My Spirit."[13]

The love of Jesus for His Father underlies all His states and
explains all His mysteries.

3. The distinction of Persons

W E can only understand the words of Jesus concerning the Holy
Spirit if we first recall what revelation teaches us of the life of this
Spirit in the Holy Trinity. You already know this mystery, but in
contemplating it anew, your faith will find an increase of joy. Let us
then penetrate, with the deepest reverence, into the very sanctuary
of divinity.

What does faith tell us? That there is in God, the Father, the Son,
and the Holy Spirit; three distinct Persons in one and the same unity
of nature.

As you know, the Father proceeds from none. He is the Principle
without principle, the first Principle of all intimate life in God, the
first origin of all the ineffable communications in the most Holy
Trinity. The Father, knowing Himself, begets by an infinite Word,
a Son, only-begotten and perfect, to whom He communicates all
that is His, all that He is, except the personal property of being the
Father. " For as the Father has life in himself, even so he has given
to the Son also to have life in himself."[1]

The Son is equal in all things to the Father. He is the adequate
expression, the perfect image of the Father. He possesses with the
Father the same divine nature. The Father and the Son give themselves, the one to the other, with a perfect love, and it is from this
gift of love from the Father to the Son, and from the Son to the
Father, that proceeds, in a mysterious manner, the Holy Spirit, the
third Person. The Holy Spirit terminates the cycle of the intimate
operations in God; He is the final term of the divine communications
in the adorable Trinity.

Between these distinct Persons, as you likewise know, there is

[13] Luke 23 :46. Christ in His mysteries, chapter XVII, section 1.
[1] John 5 :26.

B

neither superiority nor inferiority; it would be a grave error to believe that there is. These Divine Persons are equal in power, wisdom and goodness, because all Three equally possess, in an indivisible manner, one and the same divine nature with all its infinite perfection. And therefore, all our praise is addressed at the same time to the Father, the Son, and the Holy Spirit. " Glory be to the Father, and to the Son, and to the Holy Spirit! "

However, if there is among them neither inequality nor dependence, there is an order of nature, of origin, marking these communications themselves. The " procession " of the Son presupposes, without there being, however, inequality of time, the Father, who is the first principle; the " procession " of the Holy Spirit presupposes the Father and the Son, of whom He is the mutual gift.

Jesus wills that all His disciples should be baptized " in the name of the Father, and of the Son, and of the Holy Spirit."[2] That is the very language of the Incarnate Word. It contains a divine reality, the intimate comprehension of which baffles our understanding; but because it is the language of Jesus, we must inviolably respect the order between the Persons of the Trinity.

And, as we must hold intact, in our doctrine and our prayer, the unity of nature, so too we must confess the distinction of Persons, this distinction which is based upon the communications that they have between themselves and their mutual relations. There is, at the same time, equality and order; there is an identical perfection and distinction of properties.

These truths constitute an ineffable mystery concerning which we can but lisp. However, Our Lord has revealed to us the existence of this mystery, and He made this revelation in His last discourse with His disciples on the eve of His death, that our " joy may be made full."[3] He himself tells us that if we are His friends, it is because He has made known to us these secrets of God's innermost life,[4] while we await the enjoyment of them in eternal happiness. And why should He reveal these secrets to us, if He, infinite Wisdom, had not judged that this revelation would be profitable to us?

But again remark that not only by His word has God revealed this order of principle, of origin, which exists in the ineffable communications of the Persons among Themselves and upon which their

[2] Matthew 28:19.   [3] John 15:11.   [4] John 15:15.

distinction is founded. He has also chosen to manifest it by His works.

Jesus tells us in the Gospel, that eternal life is to know that the Father is the true God, and that Jesus Christ is He whom the Father has sent.[5] He often says that He was "sent" by the Father.[6] This term "sent" frequently used by Christ Jesus marks the distinction of Persons. It is the Father who "sends"; it is the Son who is "sent". The order of origin that exists from all eternity in heaven between the Father and the Son, is also manifested in time. For Christ tells us in the same place, in speaking of His Father, "I and the Father are one."[7] And again He says, addressing the Father, "All my things are thine, and thine are mine."[8] This applies to Christ considered as a divine Person; for the humanity of Jesus considered in itself, as nature, is created and consequently inferior. It is in this latter sense that Jesus says in another place, "The Father is greater than I."[9]

Jesus uses the same term "send" in speaking of the Holy Spirit. He says to the Apostles that His Father will send them the Holy Spirit. "The Advocate, the Holy Spirit, whom the Father will send in my name . . ."[10] He also says that He Himself will send Him. "But if I go, I will send Him to you."[11] As you see, it is the Father and the Son who send; it is thus Our Lord speaks of the Spirit, thereby denoting the order that exists in God in the "procession" of the Holy Spirit.

4. The Holy Spirit in the Trinity

ALL we know about the Holy Spirit is what has been taught us by Revelation. And what has it taught us?

It belongs to the infinite Essence to be one God in three Persons: the Father, Son, and Holy Spirit. That is the mystery of the most holy Trinity. Faith confesses in God both unity of nature and distinction of Persons.

---

[5] John 17:3.   [6] John 3:17; 4:34; 6:29, etc.   [7] John 10:30.
[8] John 17:40.   [9] John 14:28.   [10] John 14:26.
[11] John 16:7.   Christ the Life of the Soul, chapter VI, section 1.

The Father, in knowing Himself, declares and expresses this knowledge in the infinite Word; this act is simple and eternal; and the Son, begotten of the Father, is like and equal to Him, because the Father communicates to the Son, His nature, His life, and His perfections.

The Father and Son are drawn to one another by a common and mutual love: the Father is of such absolute perfection and beauty, the Son is so perfect an image of His Father! Thus each gives Himself to the Other, and this mutual love which springs from the Father and the Son as from one source is, in God, a subsisting love, a Person distinct from the other two Persons, named the Holy Spirit. The name is mysterious, but Revelation gives us no other.

The Holy Spirit is the ultimate term in the interior operations of the Divine life: He achieves, if we may thus lisp in speaking of such mysteries, the cycle of intimate activity in the Holy Trinity. But like the Father and the Son, He is God; He possesses, like Them and with Them, one and the same Divine nature, equal knowledge, equal power, equal majesty, equal goodness.

This Divine Spirit is named Holy; He is the Spirit of holiness—holy in Himself, He makes holy. In announcing the mystery of the Incarnation, the angel said to the Blessed Virgin, "The Holy Spirit shall come upon thee and the power of the Most High shall over-shadow thee; and therefore the Holy One to be born shall be called the Son of God."[1] Works of sanctification are especially attributed to the Holy Spirit. To understand this and all that will be said of the Holy Spirit, I must explain briefly what is called in theology "appropriation".

As you know, there is, in God, only one intelligence, only one will, only one power, because there is only one Divine nature; but also there is distinction of persons. This distinction results from the mysterious operation that are accomplished in the intimate life of God and from the mutual relations derived from these operations.

The Father begets the Son, and the Holy Spirit proceeds from the Father and the Son. "To beget," to be a Father, is the exclusive property of the First Person; "to be Son," is the personal property of the Son, as "to proceed from the Father and the Son by way of love" is the personal property of the Holy Spirit.

These personal properties establish the mutual relations between

[1] Luke 1:35.

the Father, the Son and the Holy Spirit, from whence the distinction arises. But setting apart these properties and these relations, all
is common to the Three Persons and indivisible among them: the
same intelligence, the same will, the same power, the same majesty,
because the same indivisible Divine nature is common to the Three
Persons. That is what we may know of the intimate operations in
God.

As to what concerns the "exterior" works, the actions accomplished "outside" God, whether in the material world, as the action
of directing every creature towards its end, or in the world of souls,
such as the action of producing grace, these are common to the three
Divine Persons. Why so? Because the source of these operations,
works and actions is the Divine nature and this Divine nature is, for
the Three Persons, one and indivisible; the Holy Trinity acts in the
world as one and the same Cause.

But it is God's will that men should confess and honour not only
the Divine Unity but also the Trinity of Persons. That is why the
Church, for example in her liturgy, attributes to one or other of the
Divine Persons certain actions which are produced in the world and,
although common to the Three Persons, have a special relation or an
intimate affinity with the place, if I may so speak, which this Person
occupies in the Holy Trinity and with the attributes which are
particularly and exclusively His own.

Thus, the Father being the source, origin and principle of the two
other Persons—without this implying either hierarchical superiority
or priority of time—the works produced in the world that especially
manifest power or the character of origin are attributed to the Father.
For example, the creation by which God drew the universe out of
nothing as we sing in the *Credo*: "I believe in God the Father
Almighty, Creator of heaven and earth." Had therefore the Father
a greater part, did He manifest more power in this work than the
Son and the Holy Spirit? No, it would be an error to suppose so; the
Son and the Holy Spirit acted in this as much as the Father, for God
works eternally by His almighty power, and almighty power is
common to the Three Persons.

Why then does Holy Church speak after this manner? Because
in the Holy Trinity, the Father is the *first* Person, the Principle
without principle, whence proceed the two other Persons. This is
His exclusive personal property distinguishing Him from the Son

and the Holy Spirit. It is in order that we may not forget this property that the "exterior" actions which, by affinity of nature, place it in relief, are attributed to the Father.

It is the same for the Person of the Son. He is, in the Holy Trinity, the Word proceeding from the Father by way of intelligence; He is the infinite expression of the Divine Thought; He is above all considered as Eternal Wisdom. That is why those works in which wisdom especially shine forth are attributed to Him.

It is again the same for the Holy Spirit. What is He in the Holy Trinity? He is the ultimate term of the Divine operations, of the life of God in Himself; He closes, so to speak, the cycle of the intimate Divine life: it is His personal property to proceed from both the Father and the Son by way of love. This is why all that is a work of achievement, of perfection, all that is a work of love, of union and consequently of holiness—for our holiness is measured by our degree of union with God—is attributed to the Holy Spirit.

Is it because He sanctifies more than the Father and the Son? No, the work of our sanctification is common to the Three Divine Persons; but, once again, as the work of sanctification in the soul is a work of perfecting, of achievement and union, it is attributed to the Holy Spirit because in this way we more easily remember what are His personal properties so as to honour and adore Him in that which distinguishes Him from the Father and the Son.

God wills that we should have it as much at heart to honour His Trinity of Persons as to adore His unity of nature, and therefore He wills that the Church, even in her language, should recall to the minds of her children not only that there is one God but also that He is in three Persons.

This is what is called "appropriation". It is founded on revelation and it is employed by the Church. In his encyclical letter on the Holy Spirit, Pope Leo XIII says this is done "most aptly" by the Church. It has for its aim to place in relief the attributes proper to each Divine Person. In doing this, it makes these properties known to us and makes us love them more. St. Thomas says it is to help our faith that the Church, following Revelation in this, observes the law of appropriation.[2]

During all eternity, our life, our beatitude will be to contemplate God, to love and enjoy Him, as He truly is, that is to say in the unity

[2] 1a, q.39, a.7.

of His nature and the trinity of His Persons. What is there astonishing in the fact that God, who predestines us to this life and prepares this beatitude for us, should will that, even here below, we should remember His divine perfections, as much those of His nature as the properties that distinguish the Persons. God is infinite and worthy of praise in His unity, He is equally so in His trinity; and the Divine Persons are as admirable in the unity of nature which They possess in an indivisible manner, as in the relations They have with each other and on which their distinction is founded.

"Almighty God, Eternal God, Blessed God, I rejoice in Thy almighty power, Thy eternity and Thy blessedness. When shall I behold Thee, O Principle without principle! When shall I behold Thy Son, equal to Thyself, coming forth from Thy bosom! When shall I behold Thy Holy Spirit proceeding from this union, being the term of Thy fruitfulness and consummating Thy eternal action!"[3]

5. Holy, Holy, Holy!

HUMAN reason can arrive at establishing the existence of holiness in the Supreme Being, holiness which is an attribute, a perfection of the divine nature considered in itself.

But revelation brings us a new light.

Here we must reverently raise the eyes of our soul even to the sanctuary of the adorable Trinity. We must hear what Jesus Christ, both to nourish our piety and to exercise our faith, has willed to reveal to us, or to teach us through His Church, about the intimate life of God.

There are, as you know, three Divine Persons in God, the Father, the Son, and the Holy Spirit, three distinct Persons, but all three having one and the same Nature or divine essence.

Being infinite Intelligence, the Father perfectly expresses His perfections; He expresses this knowledge in one Word, the living, substantial Word, the adequate expression of what the Father is. In uttering this Word, the Father begets the Son, to whom He communicates all His essence, all His nature, all His perfections, His

[3] Bossuet, *Preparation for Death*, 4th prayer.
Christ the Life of the Soul, chapter 1, section 3.

Life. " For as the Father has life in himself, even so he has given to
the Son also to have life in himself."[1]

The Son also belongs entirely to His Father, is entirely given up
to Him by a total donation which pertains to His nature as Son.
And from this mutual donation of one and the same love, proceeds,
as from one principle, the Holy Spirit who seals the union of the
Father and the Son by being their substantial and living love.

This mutual communication of the three Persons, this infinite
loving union between themselves assuredly constitutes a new revelation of holiness in God. It is the ineffable union of God with Himself in the unity of His nature and the trinity of Persons.[2]

Each person of the most holy Trinity is identical with the divine
Essence and consequently is holy, with a substantial holiness, because
each One acts only conformably to this Essence considered as the
supreme norm of life and activity. It may be added that the Persons
are holy because each of Them gives Himself to, and belongs to, the
Other in an act of infinite adhesion.

Finally, the Third Person is especially called " holy " because He
proceeds from the Two Others through love. Love is the principal
act by which the will tends toward its end and is united to it. It
designates the most eminent act of adhesion to the norm of all goodness; that is to say, of holiness, and therefore the Spirit, Who, in
God, proceeds through love, bears pre-eminently the name of
" Holy."[3] It is to be seen from all of this that we gain a more profound conception of Divine sanctity by considering the Trinity of
Persons.

God finds all His essential beatitude in this inexpressibly unique
and fruitful life. To exist, God has only need of Himself and all
His infinite perfections. Finding all felicity in the perfections of His
nature, and in the ineffable society of His Persons, He has no need
of any creature. He refers to Himself, in Himself, in His Trinity,
the glory which springs from His infinite perfections.

God has decreed, as you know, to make us enter into participation
of this intimate life proper to Himself alone. He wills to communicate to us this infinite, endless beatitude, which has its source in the
fullness of the infinite Being.

[1] John 5:26.
[2] Bishop Fulton Sheen treats of this at length, with great beauty, in his book *The
Divine Romance*.
[3] St. Thomas, *Opuscula selecta*, t.3, c.47.

Therefore—and this is the point of St. Paul's exposition of the Divine Plan—our holiness is to consist in adhering to God, known and loved, not only as the Author of creation, but as He knows and loves Himself in the bliss of His Trinity. This is to be united to God to the point of sharing His intimate life. In adopting us, in giving us grace, God penetrates to the depths of our nature; without changing what is essential to the order of this nature, He raises it by this grace to the point of making us truly children of God. God has decreed from all eternity that we shall only be holy in His sight by living through grace as children of God.[4]

This is the marvellous manner in which God realizes His design. Let us for a moment consider the greatness of the gift He makes us. We shall get some idea of it if we look at what takes place in the natural order.

Look at minerals; they do not live. There is no interior principle in them as the source of activity. They possess a participation in being, with certain properties, but their mode of being is very inferior. Then there is the vegetable kingdom. Plants grow and live in accordance with fixed laws, and progress towards the perfection of their being, but this life is at the bottom of the scale, for the plant is destitute of knowledge.

Although superior to that of plants, the life of animals is yet limited to sensibility and the necessities of the instinct. With man we rise to a higher sphere. Reason and free will characterize the life proper to a human being. But man is also matter. Above him is the angel, a pure spirit, whose life reaches the highest degree in the scale of creation.

Infinitely surpassing all these created lives received in participation, is the Divine Life, life uncreated, fully autonomous and independent, above the strength of any creature, a necessary life, subsistent in itself. God being unlimited intelligence, apprehends by an eternal act, both the infinite and every being of which the prototype is found in Him. Being the sovereign Will, He attaches Himself in the fullness of His strength to the Supreme Good, which is none other than Himself. In this Divine life in which is all plenitude, is found the source of all perfection and the principle of all bliss.

It is this life which God wills to communicate to us. It is a share in this life which forms our holiness. And as, for us, there are degrees

---

[4] This actually is the theme of *Christ the Life of the Soul*.

in this participation, the more this participation is extended, the higher will be our holiness.

And let us never forget that it is only out of love that God has resolved to give Himself thus. The ineffable communications of the Divine Persons with each other are all that is necessary in God.[5] These mutual relations belong to the very essence of God; it is the life of God.

All other communications that God makes of Himself are the outcome of a love supremely free. But as this love is divine, the gift of it makes us so likewise. God loves divinely; He gives Himself. We are called to receive this Divine communication in an ineffable measure. God intends to give Himself to us, not only as supreme beauty, to be the object of our contemplation, but to unite Himself to us so as to make Himself, as far as possible, one with us.

Holy Father, said Jesus at the Last Supper, let my disciples be one in Us, as Thou and I are one, so that they may find in this union the endless joy of Our own beatitude, " In order that they may have my joy made full in themselves."[6]

6. The Operations of the Holy Spirit in Christ

LET us reverently approach the divine Person of Jesus Christ that we may contemplate something of the marvels realized in Him—in the Incarnation and since the Incarnation. Let us consider the operations of the Holy Spirit in Our Lord.

The Holy Trinity created a soul which it united to a human body so as to form one human nature, and united this human nature to the divine Person of the word. The three divine Persons concurred together in this ineffable work, although it is necessary to add immediately that it had for its final term, the Word alone; only the Word, the Son, became Incarnate.

This work is then due to the entire Trinity, but it is especially

---

[5] Necessary in this sense that it is impossible for them not to be. St. Thomas, *Summa*, Ia, q.41, a.2, at 5.

[6] John 17:11, 13. Cf. John 15:11.

Christ the Life of the Soul, chapter VI, section 2.

attributed to the Holy Spirit. We say in the Creed, " I believe . . . in Jesus Christ, Our Lord, who was conceived by the Holy Spirit . . ." The *Credo* only repeats the words of the angel to the Blessed Virgin, " The Holy Spirit shall come upon thee . . . and therefore the Holy One to be born shall be called the Son of God."[1]

You will ask, perhaps, why this special attribution to the Holy Spirit? Because, among other reasons given by St. Thomas,[2] the Holy Spirit is substantial love, the love of the Father and the Son; now if the Redemption through the Incarnation is a work of which the fulfillment demanded infinite wisdom, it has however its first cause in God's love for us. " God so loved the world," Jesus Himself told us, " that he gave his only-begotten Son."[3]

And think how fruitful and wonderful the virtue of the Holy Spirit is in Christ! Not only does He unite the human nature to the Word but to Him is attributed the effusion of sanctifying grace in the soul of Jesus.

In Jesus Christ there are two distinct natures, both perfect, but united in the Person who embraces them, namely, the Word. It is the " grace of union " that causes human nature to subsist in the Divine Person of the Word. This grace is an altogether unique, transcendent and incommunicable order. Through it the humanity of Christ belongs to the Word; it has become the humanity of the true Son of God and the object of the eternal Father's infinite delight. But, the human nature, while being thus united to the Word, is not annihilated and does not remain in immobility. It retains its essence, its integrity, as likewise its energies and capacities; it is capable of action. Now, it is sanctifying grace that raises this human nature so that it can act supernaturally.

To state the same idea in other terms, the grace of hypostatic union unites the human nature to the Person of the Word and thus renders everything divine in Christ. Christ *is* by this grace a divine " subject "; this is the work of the grace of union of which the character is unique.

But it is befitting that this human nature should also be adorned with sanctifying grace in order to *operate* divinely in each of its faculties. This sanctifying grace which is connatural to the " grace of union " (that is to say, which is derived from the grace of union in a manner as it were natural) places the soul of Christ in the state

[1] Luke 1:35.   [2] 3a, q.32, a.1.   [3] John 3:16.

befitting its union with the Word. This is done in such a way that
the human nature—which subsists in the Word by virtue of the grace
of union—can act as befits a soul raised to so eminent a dignity and
can produce Divine fruit.

Therefore, in Christ, the effect of the grace of union of which the
object is the union of the human nature with the Person of the Word,
is different from the effect of sanctifying grace. The latter gives the
capacity of acting supernaturally to this human nature, which
remains (even after the union with the Word is accomplished)
integral in its essence and faculties. Therefore this sanctifying grace
being distinct from the grace of union, is not superfluous, as might
appear at first sight.

It is also to be observed that the grace of union is only to be found
in Christ, while sanctifying grace is likewise in the souls of the just.
In Christ sanctifying grace is in all its fullness and it is of this fullness that all receive it in a more or less extensive measure. But it is
above all necessary to observe that Christ is not the adoptive Son of
God such as we become by sanctifying grace. He is the Son of God
by nature. In us, sanctifying grace establishes divine adoption; in
Christ, the function of sanctifying grace is to act in such a way that
the human nature of Christ—once united to the Person of the Word
by the grace of union and become, by this same grace, the Humanity
of the very Son of God—is able to work in a supernatural manner.

And that is why sanctifying grace has not been given to the soul
of Christ in a limited measure as it is with the elect, but carried to its
highest degree. Now, the pouring forth of this sanctifying grace in
the soul of Christ is attributed to the Holy Spirit.

At the same time, the Holy Spirit has poured forth on the soul of
Jesus the fullness of the virtues and the fullness of His gifts. Hear
what Isaias sang of the Virgin and of the Christ who was to be born
of her, " There shall come forth a rod out of the root of Jesse (that is,
the Virgin) and a flower shall rise up out of his root (Christ). And
the Spirit of the Lord shall rest upon Him, the spirit of wisdom and
of understanding, the spirit of counsel and of fortitude, the spirit
of knowledge and of godliness. And He shall be filled with the spirit
of fear of the Lord."

In a remarkable circumstance related by St. Luke, Our Lord
applied to Himself these texts of the prophet. You know that at that
time the Jews assembled in the synagogue on the Sabbath day. A

teacher of the law chosen from among those present took the scroll of the Scriptures to read the part of the sacred text appointed for that day. St. Luke relates how, one Sabbath day, our Divine Lord, then at the beginning of His public life, entered the synagogue of Nazareth.

The book of the prophet Isaias was given into His hands and, having unfolded it, He found the place where it was written, " The Spirit of the Lord is upon Me, wherefore He has anointed me to preach the gospel to the poor, He has sent me to heal the contrite of heart, to preach deliverance to the captives . . . to preach the acceptable year of the Lord." Having folded the book, He restored it and sat down; the eyes of all in the synagogue were fixed upon Him.

Then He said to them, " Today, this scripture has been fulfilled in your hearing."[4] Our Lord made His own the words of Isaias which compared the action of the Holy Spirit to an unction.[5] The grace of the Holy Spirit is poured forth upon Jesus, like an oil of gladness which first anointed Him Son of God and the Messias, and then filled Him with the plenitude of His gifts and the abundance of divine treasures.[6] It was at the very moment of the Incarnation that this blessed unction was conferred. It was to signify this, to manifest it to the Jews, to proclaim that He is the Messias, the Christ, that is to say, the Lord Anointed, that the Holy Spirit visible descended upon Jesus under the form of a dove on the day of His baptism when the Incarnate Word was to begin His public life. It was indeed by this sign that Christ was to be recognized, as was declared by His Precursor, St. John the Baptist, " He upon whom thou wilt see the Spirit descending and abiding upon Him, He it is who baptizes with the Holy Spirit."[7]

From this moment, the Evangelists show us that in all things the Soul of Christ is directed by the Holy Spirit and His activity inspired by Him. It is the Holy Spirit who leads Him into the desert to be tempted,[8] and after His sojourn in the desert it is in the power of the Spirit that He returns to Galilee.[9] By the action of this same Spirit He casts out devils[10] and under the action of the Holy Spirit He rejoices when He thanks His Father for revealing His divine secrets to the little ones.[11]

[4] Luke 4:16.   [5] The hymn " Veni Creator Spiritus ".   [6] Ps. 44:5.
[7] John 1:33.   [8] Matt. 4:1.   [9] Luke 4:14.
[10] Matt. 12:28.   [11] Luke 10:21.

Finally, St. Paul tells us that in the chief work of Christ, the one in which His love for His Father and for us most shines out—namely His bloody sacrifice on the cross for the salvation of the world—it was by the Holy Spirit that Christ Himself: "Who through the Holy Spirit offered himself unblemished unto God."[12]

What do all these revelations show? That in Christ, the human activity was directed by the Spirit of love.

The One who acts is Christ, the Incarnate Word. All His actions are the actions of the One Person of the Word in whom the human nature subsists; but it is under the inspiration, by the promptings of the Holy Spirit, that Christ acted. The human soul of Jesus had, through the grace of the hypostatic union, become the soul of the Word; it was filled like to none other with sanctifying grace, and lastly, it acted under the guidance of the Holy Spirit.

And this is why all the actions of Christ Jesus were holy. Certainly His soul is created, like every other soul; but it was all-holy, first because it is united to the Word; it is thus constituted, from the first moment of the Incarnation, in a state of union with a Divine Person which makes it not merely the soul of a saint, but of the Saint of saints, the very Son of God. It is holy, too, because it is adorned with sanctifying grace which makes it capable of acting supernaturally, and in a manner worthy of the supreme union which constitutes its inalienable privilege. In fine, it is holy because all its actions, all its operations, although being and remaining the actions of the one Incarnate Word, are wrought through the movement, under the inspiration of the Holy Spirit, the Spirit of Love, the Spirit of Holiness.

Let us adore these marvels produced in Christ: the Holy Spirit renders holy the being and activity of Christ; and because, in Christ, this holiness attains the supreme degree, because all human holiness is to be modelled upon it and must be subject to it, the Church sings daily in the *Gloria* of the Mass, "Thou only art holy" O Christ Jesus. Only Thou art holy because only Thou art by Thy Incarnation the true Son of God; only holy, because Thou possessest sanctifying grace in its fullness that so Thou mayest distribute it to us; only holy because Thy soul was infinitely docile to the promptings of the Spirit of Love Who inspired and ruled all Thy movements, all Thy acts and made them pleasing to Thy Father.

[12] Hebrews 9:14.

7. The Holy Spirit
and the Mysteries of Christ

"I F you loved me," said Christ Jesus to his apostles, "you would indeed rejoice that I am going to the Father."[1] For those who love Christ, the Ascension is, indeed, an inexhaustible source of joy. It is the supreme glorification of Jesus to the highest heavens. It is the realization of that prayer of Christ, "And now do thou, Father, glorify me with thyself, with the glory I had with thee before the world existed."[2] We are full of gladness in contemplating Jesus, the Son of God, our Redeemer, our Head, sitting at the right hand of His Father, after having fulfilled here below, in the self-abasement of His Incarnation and the humiliations of His death, His mission of salvation.

But Our Lord did not only say to His disciples that they ought to rejoice in His Ascension. He added that His Ascension would profit them. "But I speak the truth to you; it is expedient for you that I depart, For if I do not go, the Advocate will not come to you; but if I go I will send Him to you."[3]

All the utterances of the Incarnate Word are, as He Himself says, "spirit and life."[4] They are deep and solemn, sometimes mysterious; there are some that are difficult to understand, and can hardly be fathomed except in prayer. The word of Jesus which we have just quoted on the subject of His leaving the world is one of these utterances.

"It is expedient for you that I go."[5] How can it be good for the Apostles that Jesus shall go? That He shall leave them, to ascend to to His Father? Is He not for them the source of every good, of every grace? Is He not "The Way, the Truth and the Life"?[6] and did He not say, "No one comes to the Father but through me."? How then can it be useful to the disciples for Jesus to leave them?

Might they not have answered Him in all truth: O Divine Master, say not so; we need none other save You; You are sufficient for us.

Christ in His mysteries, chapter XVII, introduction.

[1] John 14:28.
[2] John 17:5.
[3] John 16:7.
[4] John 6:64.
[5] John 16:7.
[6] John 14:6.

To whom shall we go?[7] With you have we not every grace? Abide then with us.[8]

But the Divine Master's words are formal. "I tell you the truth—it is expedient for you that I depart. For if I do not go, the Advocate will not come to you."

This is the mystery, and it is this mystery that we are about to contemplate, as far as is possible for us. For here, all is supernatural, and faith alone can be our guide.

The visible mission of the Holy Spirit to the disciples, the mission that constitutes the special object of the solemnity of Pentecost, belongs to Jesus, in His divine nature, (as it belongs also to the Father), and that it enters on this account into the cycle of Christ's mysteries.

Christ Jesus *prayed* for this mission. He made it the object of a special demand. Our Lord said to His disciples at the Last Supper, "And I will ask the Father and He will give you another Advocate to dwell with you forever."[9]

Besides, Jesus *promised* His apostles to send them this Consoler. "But when the Advocate has come, whom I will send you from the Father, the Spirit of Truth who proceeds from the Father, he will bear witness concerning me . . . If I go, I will send Him to you."[10]

Our Lord, moreover, *merited* this mission. By His prayer, as by His sacrifice, Christ Jesus obtained from the Father that the Spirit of truth, of love, of fortitude and of consolation should be given to them. We owe every grace to the prayer and immolation of the Saviour, as was wonderfully verified in the coming of this Spirit, so powerful and so full of goodness that Jesus Himself declares Him His equal, in Whom the apostles were to find another Himself.

Finally, above all, the sending of the Holy Spirit to the apostles has no other end, as you know, than to achieve the *establishment* of the Church. Jesus had founded this Church upon Peter, but He left to the Holy Spirit (and we shall see why in another place) the care of bringing it to perfection.

Indeed, before His Ascension, being at table with His apostles, He told them "not to depart from Jerusalem, but to wait for the promise of the Father."[11] The coming of this Spirit was to serve for the glorification of Jesus; at the same time, the Spirit would fill them

---

[7] John 6:69.   [8] Luke 24:29.   [9] John 14:16-17.
[10] John 15:26; 16:7.   [11] Acts 1:4.

with power whereby they should render testimony to Jesus in the holy city "and in all Judea and Samaria and even to the very ends of the earth."[12] These are Jesus Christ's own words.

Then, as you see, this mission of the Holy Spirit to the Apostles truly belongs to Jesus. This is so true that St. Paul calls the Holy Spirit, "the Spirit of Christ," the Spirit of Jesus.[13] This is why we can never go through the cycle of Christ's mysteries without contemplating this marvellous work which was wrought ten days after the Ascension.

Let us then implore the Holy Spirit Himself to make known to us what He is, in what His mission and work consists on the day of Pentecost. "Come Spirit of Truth, enlighten our minds so that the flame of love of which thou art the infinite source may be enkindled in our hearts. Perfect in us an ever-new Pentecost! "

8. The Work of Pentecost Day

JESUS told His apostles that after He had returned to heaven, He would send them the Holy Spirit.

In His divine nature, Jesus is, with the Father, the principle from which the Holy Spirit proceeds. The gift of the Holy Spirit to the Church and to souls is a priceless gift, since this Spirit is the Divine Love in Person. But this gift, like every grace, was merited for us by Jesus. It is the fruit of His Passion. He purchased it by the sufferings He endured in His sacred humanity.

Was it not therefore just that this grace should not be given to the world until that humanity whereby it had been merited, had been glorified? This exaltation of the humanity in Jesus was not accomplished in its fullness, nor did it reach its fruition until the day of the Ascension. It was only then that the sacred humanity entered definitively into possession of the glory to which it is doubly entitled as being united to the Son of God, and as a victim offered to the Father, thereby to merit every grace for souls. Seated at the right hand of the Father in the glory of heaven, the humanity of the Incarnate Word

---

[12] Acts 1:8.   [13] Romans 8:9, Acts 16:7; 1 Peter 1:11.
Christ in His mysteries, chapter XVII, sections 2 and 3.

C

was to be thus associated with the "sending" of the Holy Spirit by the Father and the Son to perform the great works of that first Pentecost.

We now understand the reason Our Lord Himself said to the Apostles: it is expedient to you that I go or the Paraclete will not come to you; but if I go, I will send Him.[1] It is as if He said: I have merited this grace for you by My Passion; in order that it may be given to you, it is first necessary that My Passion should be followed by My glory.

The Fathers of the Church add another reason, relating to the disciples, why the work of Pentecost must be preceeded by the Ascension of Our Lord.[2]

One day Jesus promised that living water should spring up in those who believed in Him. St. John the Evangelist, in relating this promise, adds, "He said this, however, of the Spirit whom they who believed in him were to receive; for the Spirit had not yet been given, seeing that Jesus had not yet been glorified."[3] Faith was, therefore, the source, so to speak, of the coming of the Holy Spirit in us.

Now as long as Christ Jesus lived upon earth, the faith of the disciples was imperfect. It would only be entire, it could only unfold in all fullness when the Ascension had taken the human presence of their Divine Master from their sight. "Because thou hast seen me, thou hast believed," said Jesus to Thomas after the resurrection. "Blessed are they who have not seen and yet have believed."[4]

"After the Ascension, the faith of the disciples, better instructed, went further and higher to seek Christ sitting near to the Father and equal to the Father."[5]

It is because the apostles' faith after the Ascension, had become purer, more interior, more intense, more efficacious, that the "river of living water" sprang up in them with such impetuosity.

We know, indeed, how magnificently Jesus fulfilled His divine promise; how ten days after the Ascension, the Holy Spirit, sent by the Father and the Son, descended upon the apostles assembled in the Cenacle, with what abundance of graces and charismata this

---

[1] John 16:7.   [2] E.G. St. Augustine, *Enarr in Psal,* 109; *Sermones* 143 and 264.
[3] John 7:39.   [4] John 20:29.   [5] St. Leo, *2nd Sermon on the Ascension,* c.4.

Spirit of truth and love was poured forth in the souls of the disciples.

What indeed was the work of the Holy Spirit in the souls of the Apostles on the day of Pentecost?

To understand it well, I ought first to recall to you the Church's teaching upon the character of divine works. You know that in the domain of the supernatural life of grace, as well as in the works of the natural creation, all that God produces outside Himself, in time, is accomplished by the Father, the Son and the Holy Spirit, without distinction of persons. The three Persons then act in the unity of their divine nature. The distinction of Persons exists only in the incomprehensible communications that constitute the innermost life of God in Himself.

But in order to remind ourselves more easily of these revelations concerning the Divine Persons, the Church, in her language, attributes specially such or such action to one of the three Persons, on account of the affinity that exists between this action and the exclusive properties whereby this Person is distinguished from the others.

Thus the Father is the first principle, proceeding from none other, but from whom proceed the Son and the Holy Spirit. Therefore the work that marks the origin of everything, the creation, is especially attributed to Him. Did the Father create alone? Certainly not. The Son and the Holy Spirit created at the same time as the Father, and in union with Him. But between the property, peculiar to the Father, of being the first principle in the divine communications and the work of creation, there is an affinity, in virtue of which the Church can, without error of doctrine, attribute the creation to the Father.

The Son, the Word, is the infinite expression of the thought of the Father. He is considered especially as Wisdom. The works in which this perfection shines forth above all, as in that of ordering the world, are particularly attributed to Him. He is indeed that Wisdom which coming forth out of the mouth of the Most High " reaching from end to end mightily and ordering all things sweetly."[6]

The Church applies the same law to the Holy Spirit. What is He in the adorable Trinity? He is the ultimate term, the consummation of life in God. He closes the intimate cycle of the admirable operations of the Divine Life. And this is why, in order that we may remember this property which is personal to Him, the Church

---

[6] Antiphon for Dec. 17.

specially attributes to Him all that which is the work of grace, of
sanctification, all that concerns the completion, the crowning-point,
the consummation: He is the Divine Artist who, by his least touches,
brings the work to its sovereign perfection.[7] The work attributed to
the Holy Spirit, in the Church as in souls, is to lead to its end, to its
term, to its ultimate perfection, the incessant labour of holiness.

Let us now consider, for a few moments, the divine workings of
this Spirit in the souls of the Apostles.

He fills them with truth. You will at once say: Had not Christ
Jesus done this? Certainly He had. Did He not Himself declare, " I
am the truth."[8] He came into the world to bear witness to the
truth,[9] and you know, also from Himself, that He wholly consummated His mission.[10]

Yes, but now that He has left His apostles, it is the Holy Spirit
who is about to become their interior Master. " For he will not speak
on his own authority," said Jesus, wishing to signify by this that the
Holy Spirit—proceeding from the Father and the Son, receiving
from them divine life—will give us the infinite truth that He
receives by His ineffable procession. " He will teach you all things
and bring to your mind whatever I have said to you. " " He will
glorify Me because he will receive of what is mine and declare it to
you."[11]

There is yet more. The apostles had no need to trouble about what
they should reply when the Jews delivered them up before the
tribunals, and forbade them to preach the name of Jesus; it was the
Holy Spirit who would inspire their replies.[12] And thus they should
bear witness to Jesus: " But you shall receive power when the Holy
Spirit comes upon you, and you shall be witnesses for me . . . even
to the very ends of the earth."[13]

And as it is by the tongue, the organ of speech, that testimony is
rendered, and whereby the preaching of the name of Jesus was to go
forth " to the very ends of the earth," this Spirit, on the day of
Pentecost, descends visibly upon the Apostles in the form of tongues.

But these are tongues of fire. And why? Because the Holy Spirit
comes to fill the hearts of the apostles with *love*. These are flames of
love! He is personal love in the life of God. He is, as it were, the

---

[7] Hymn *Veni Creator*.   [8] John 14:6.   [9] John 18:37.
[10] John 17:4.   [11] John 14:26; 16:13-14.
[12] Matthew 10:19-20; Mark 13:11 Luke 12.   [13] Acts 1:8.

breath, the aspiration of the infinite love from which we drew life.

It is related in Genesis that "the Lord God formed man of the slime of the earth and breathed into his face the breath of life."[14] This vital breath was the symbol of the Spirit to whom we owe the supernatural life. On the day of Pentecost, the Divine Spirit brought such an abundance of life to all the Church that to signify it, "suddenly there came a sound from heaven, as of a violent wind coming, and it filled the whole house where they were sitting."[15]

In descending upon them, the Holy Spirit pours forth in them His love which is Himself. It was needful that the Apostles should be filled with love in order that in preaching the name of Jesus they should give birth to the love of their Master in the souls of their hearers. It was necessary that their testimony, dictated by the Spirit, should be so full of life as to attach the world to Jesus Christ.

Moreover, this love, ardent as a flame, powerful as a tempestuous wind, is necessary to the Apostles in order that they may be able to meet the dangers foretold by Christ when they shall have preached His holy Name. The Holy Spirit fills them with *fortitude*.

Look at St. Peter, the prince of the Apostles. On the eve of the Passion of Jesus, he promises to follow Him even unto death. But that same night, at the voice of a servant, he denies His Master; he swears that he knows not the man[16] See him now, on the day of Pentecost. He announces Christ to thousands of Jews. He reproaches them freely for having crucified Him. He bears witness to His Resurrection, and earnestly exhorts them to "repent and be baptized."[17] It is no longer the timid disciple who fears danger and follows afar off;[18] he is the witness who declares before all and in firm and bold words, that Christ is the Son of God.

What power in Peter's words! The Apostle is no longer recognizable. The virtue of the Holy Spirit has changed him, the love that he bears towards His Master is henceforward strong and generous. Our Lord Himself had foretold this transformation when He said to His disciples before ascending into heaven, "But wait here in the city, until you are clothed with power from on high."[19]

Again, see this same St. Peter and the other Apostles, a few days after the event. Notice how the Jews are moved by their words, by the miracles they work, and the conversions that they bring about in

[14] Genesis 2:7.   [15] Acts 2:2.   [16] Matthew 26:74; Mark 14:71.
[17] Acts 2:23-24, 38.   [18] Mark 14:54.   [19] Luke 24:49.

the name of Jesus. The chief priests and the Sadducees who brought
about Christ's death, forbid His disciples to preach the Saviour. You
know their reply "Whether it is right in the sight of God to listen
to you rather than to God, decide for yourselves. For we cannot but
speak of what we have seen and heard."[20]

What is it that makes them speak with such courage, they who, on
the night of the Passion, forsook Jesus; who during the days that
followed the Resurrection, remained hidden with the doors fast shut,
"for fear of the Jews."[21] It is the Spirit of truth, the Spirit of love,
the Spirit of fortitude.

It is because their love for Christ is strong that they deliver themselves up to torments, for the Jewish officials, seeing that the Apostles
pay no heed to their prohibition, bring them before the council. But
St. Peter declares in the name of all that they "must obey God rather
than men."[22]

You know what happened then. To overcome this constancy, they
scourged the Apostles before releasing them. But note what the
sacred writer adds. On going forth from the council the Apostles
rejoiced "that they had been counted worthy to suffer disgrace for
the name of Jesus."[23] And where did it come from, this joy in
suffering and humiliations? From the Holy Spirit, for He is not only
the Spirit of fortitude, He is also the Spirit of Consolation, "I will
ask the Father," says Jesus and He will give you another Advocate
. . . the Spirit of truth."[24]

Is not Christ Jesus Himself already a Consoler, an Advocate?
Certainly He is; did He not say, "Come to me, all you who labour
and are burdened, and I will give you rest."[25] Is He not, as St. Paul
has revealed to us, a High Priest who knows how to have compas-
sion on our sufferings, because He has Himself passed through
suffering?[26]

But this Divine Consoler was to disappear from the earthly eyes
of the disciples. That is why He asked His Father to send them
another Consoler, equal to Himself, God like Himself.

Because He is the Spirit of truth, this Consoler assuages the needs
of our intelligence; because He is the Spirit of love, He satisfies the
desires of our heart; because He is the Spirit of strength, He sustains

[20] Acts 4:18-20.   [21] John 20:19.   [22] Acts 5:29.
[23] Acts 5:41.   [24] John 14:16-17.   [25] Matthew 11:28.
[26] Hebrews 4:15; 5:2.

us in our toils, trials and tears. The Holy Spirit is eminently the Consoler. His work began on Pentecost and reaped its first harvest in the souls of the Apostles.

"Oh! Come and dwell in us, Father of the poor, Giver of heavenly gifts, Thou best consoler, sweet guest, and refreshment full of sweetness for the soul."[27]

9. The Holy Spirit in the Church

THE marvels which operated in Christ under the inspiration of the Spirit are reproduced in us, at least in part, when we allow ourselves to be guided by this Divine Spirit. But do we possess this Spirit? Yes, without any doubt.

Before ascending into Heaven, Jesus promised His disciples that He would ask the Father to give them the Holy Spirit. He made the gift of this Spirit to our souls the object of a special prayer. "I will ask the Father and He will give you another Advocate to dwell with you forever, the Spirit of truth."[1]

You know how the prayer of Jesus was granted and how abundantly the Holy Spirit was given to the Apostles on the day of Pentecost. This marvel marked, as it were, the taking possession of the Church, Christ's mystical body, by the Divine Spirit. We may say that if Christ is the Chief, the Head of the Church, the Holy Spirit is the soul of it. It is the Holy Spirit who guides and inspires the Church, keeping her, as Jesus said, in the truth of Christ and in the light He has brought us. "But the Advocate . . . will teach you all things and bring to your mind whatever I have said to you."[2]

This action of the Holy Spirit in the Church is varied and manifold. I have said elsewhere that Christ was anointed Messias and High Priest by an ineffable unction of the Holy Spirit; all those whom Christ wills to make participants of His priestly power that so they may continue here below His sanctifying mission, are made partakers of it by the unction of the Holy Spirit. "Receive the Holy

[27] Sequence *Veni Sancte Spiritus*.
Christ the Life of the Soul, chapter VI, section 3.
[1] John 14:16-17.   [2] John 14:26.

Spirit"[3] about the power to forgive sins and " The Holy Spirit has placed you as bishops to rule the Church of God."[4]

It is the Holy Spirit who speaks by their mouth and gives value to their testimony.[5] In the same way, the authentic means that Christ has given to his ministers, whereby they may transmit life to souls, namely the Sacraments, are never conferred without the Holy Spirit being invoked. It is He who fructifies the waters of Baptism; it is necessary to "be born again of water and the Holy Spirit" to enter into the Kingdom of God.[6] St. Paul says that God saves us "through the bath of regeneration and renewal by the Holy Spirit."[7]

In Confirmation, the Holy Spirit is " given" to be the unction which is to make the Christian a valiant soldier of Jesus Christ; it is the Holy Spirit Who, in this sacrament, gives us the fullness of the state of Christian and clothes us in Christ's own strength. It is to the Holy Spirit, as is especially shown in the Eastern liturgy, that the change is attributed whereby the bread and wine become the Body and Blood of Christ. Sins are forgiven in the sacrament of Penance by the Holy Spirit.[8] In Extreme Unction He is besought that His grace may cure the sick of their languors and sins. In the Sacrament of Matrimony the Holy Spirit is invoked in order that the Christian bridegroom and bride may, by their lives, imitate the union that exists between Christ and the Church.

Do you not see how full of life, how penetrating and constant, is the action of the Holy Spirit in the Church? Yes, He is indeed, as St. Paul says, " the Spirit of life "[9], a truth the Church repeats in the Creed when she chants " the Holy Spirit, the life-giver." He is truly the soul of the Church; He is the vital principle animating and governing her, uniting all her members one with another and giving them spiritual strength and beauty.[10]

The Holy Spirit is truly the soul of the Church. When was say that the Holy Spirit is the soul of the Church, we evidently do not intend to say that He is the form of the Church, as the soul is, in us, the form of the body. Taking things from this point of view, it would be more theologically correct to say that the soul of the Church is sanctifying grace (with the infused virtues that are necessarily attend-

---

[3] John 20:22.   [4] Acts 20:28.   [5] John 15:26; Acts 15:28; 20:22-28.
[6] John 3:5.   [7] Titus 3:5.   [8] John 20:22-23.
[9] Rom. 8:2.   [10] St. Augustine. Sermon 187 de tempore.

ant upon it); grace is, in fact, the principle of supernatural life, which makes the members belonging to the Body of the Church live with Divine life.

However, even then, the analogy between grace and the soul is only imperfect; but this is not the moment to dwell on these distinctions. When we say that the Holy Spirit and not grace, is the soul of the Church, we indicate the cause instead of the effect, for it is the Holy Spirit who produces sanctifying grace. We wish then by this expression (the Holy Spirit is the soul of the Church) to mark the inward influence, vivifying and " unifying ", if one may thus express it, that the Holy Spirit exercises in the Church.

This manner of speaking is perfectly legitimate; it is employed by several of the Fathers of the Church (notably St. Augustine). Some modern theologians use the expression and Pope Leo XIII has consecrated this expression in his encyclical on the Holy Spirit. It is interesting to remark that St. Thomas, in order to denote the internal influence of the Holy Spirit in the Church, compares it to that which the heart exercises in the human organism.

In the first days of the Church's existence, this action of the Holy Spirit was much more visible than in our own days. It entered into the designs of Providence, for it was necessary that the Church should be firmly established by manifesting, in the sight of the pagan world, striking signs of the Divinity of her Founder, of her origin and mission.

These signs, the fruits of the out-pouring of the Holy Spirit, were wonderful. We marvel when we read the account of the beginnings of the Church. The Holy Spirit descended upon those who through baptism were made Christ's disciples. He filled them with " charismata " as numerous as they were astonishing: graces of miracles, gifts of prophecy, gifts of tongues and many other extraordinary favours granted to the first Christians in order that the Church, adorned with such an abundance of eminent gifts might be recognized as the true Church of Jesus.

Read in St. Paul's first letter to the Corinthians how the great Apostle rejoices in enumerating these marvels of which he was himself a witness. At almost each enumeration of these gifts, he adds: but it is " the same Spirit " who is the source of them, because He is Love, and love is the principle of all these gifts.[11] He it is who makes

[11] I Cor. 12:9 ff.

fruitful this Church which Jesus has redeemed by His blood that it might "be holy and without blemish."[12]

10. The continuing Pentecost

THE Holy Spirit came for us. Those assembled in the Cenacle on the first Pentecost represented all the Church. The Spirit comes that He may abide with her forever, This is Christ's own promise: He will "dwell with you forever."[1]

The Holy Spirit descended visibly upon the Apostles at Pentecost; from that day, Holy Church has been spreading over all the earth. She is the kingdom of Jesus, and it is the Holy Spirit who, with the Father and the Son, governs His Kingdom. He completes in souls the work of holiness begun by the redemption. He is, in the Church, what the soul is to the body: the Spirit that animates and quickens it, the Spirit that safeguards unity, while His action produces manifold and diverse effects. He brings all her vigour and beauty.

See indeed what abundance of grace and charismata inundate the Church on Pentecost. We read in the *Acts of the Apostles,* the book which is the history of the beginning of the Church, that the Holy Spirit came down visibly upon those who were baptized and that He filled them with marvellous graces. With what complacency St. Paul enumerates them: "Now there are varieties of gifts, but the same Spirit . . . who works all things in all. Now the manifestation of the Spirit is given to everyone for profit. To one through the Spirit is given utterance of wisdom and to another the utterance of knowledge, according to the same Spirit; to another the gift of healing, in the one Spirit; to another the working of miracles; to another prophecy; to another the distinguishing of spirits; to another various kinds of tongues." And the Apostle adds, "But all these things are the work of one and the same Spirit, who divides to everyone according as he will."[2]

It is the Holy Spirit, promised and sent by the Father and Jesus, who gave this plenitude and this intensity of supernatural life to the first Christians. Dissimilar as they were, they had however, on

---

[12] Ephes. 5:27.   Christ in His mysteries, chapter XVII, section 4.
[1] John 14:16.   [2] Cor. 12:4-11.

account of the love that the Holy Spirit poured forth in them "one heart and one soul."[3]

Since then, the Holy Spirit abides in the Church in a permanent, indefectible manner, therein exercising an unceasing action of life and sanctification. "He will dwell with you and be in you."[4] He renders her infallible in the truth: "But when he, the Spirit of truth, has come, he will teach you all truth,"[5] and will guard you from error. By His action a wonderful supernatural fruitfulness springs up in the Church. He plants and unfolds in virgins, martyrs, and confessors, those heroic virtues which are among the marks of holiness. In a word, He is the Spirit who by His inspirations, works in souls, rendering the Church which Jesus acquired for Himself by His most precious Blood—holy and without blemish, worthy of being presented by Christ to His Father, on the day of final triumph.

Historically, and as a visible mission, Pentecost is doubtless ended, but the inward action of the Spirit is unceasing. Its virtue endures for ever; its grace remains. The Holy Spirit's mission in souls is henceforth invisible, but it is none the less fruitful.

Look at the Church on the day when she celebrates the Ascension. What is her prayer, after having sung the glorification of her divine Bridegroom and having rejoiced with gladness over His triumph? "O King of glory, Lord of hosts, who did today ascend in triumph to the highest heavens, leave us not orphans, but send down upon us the Spirit of truth promised by the Father."[6]

O most powerful High Priest, now that thou art seated at the right hand of the Father, and dost enjoy in all fullness Thy victory and power, ask Thy Father as Thou didst promise, to send us another Comforter. By the sufferings of Thy humanity, Thou didst merit this grace for us. The Father will hear Thee because He loves Thee. Because Thou art His beloved Son, He will send with Thee the Spirit that He Himself promised through the prophets when He said, "I will pour forth the Spirit of grace and of prayer upon all the inhabitants of Jerusalem." Send Him into our souls, that He may abide there forever.

The Church prays as if Pentecost was to be renewed for us. She repeats the antiphon "O King of glory . . ." each day during the octave of the Ascension; then, on the day of the solemnity of Pente-

---

[3] Acts 4:32.　　　[4] John 14:17.　　　[5] John 16:13.
[6] Antiphon from 2nd Vespers of the Ascension.

cost, she multiplies the praises she offers to the Spirit in language full of magnificence and poetry. "Come Holy Spirit, fill the hearts of Thy faithful and kindle in the fire of love.[7] Come from the height of heaven, send down on us a ray of Thy light! O most blessed light, fill our inmost hearts with Thy radiance![8] Fount of living water, Fire of love, spiritual Unction, come! Shed Thy light in our minds, pour forth Thy charity into our hearts, strengthen our weakness with Thy unfailing strength![9]

If the Church, our Mother, places these desires in our souls and these prayers upon our lips, it is not only to recall to us the visible mission which took place on Pentecost but in order that this mystery may be interiorly renewed within us all.

Let us repeat these ardent aspirations with the Church. Above all, let us beseech the heavenly Father to send us this Spirit. Through sanctifying grace, we are His children, and, as such, our condition urges the Father to pour down His gifts upon us. It is because He loves us as His children that He gives us His Son. Holy Communion is "the Bread of children."[10] Again, it is because we are His children that He sends us His Spirit, one of His most perfect gifts.[11]

Indeed, what does St. Paul say? "And because you are sons, God has sent the Spirit of His Son into our hearts."[12] He is the Spirit of the Son because He proceeds from the Son as from the Father, and He is sent by both the Father and the Son. This is why, in the preface for Pentecost, the Church sings, "It is truly meet and just . . . that we always and in all places, give thanks to Thee, O holy Lord, Father Almighty, eternal God, through Christ Our Lord. Who, ascending above all the heavens, and sitting at Thy right hand, did this day send down upon the children of adoption the Holy Spirit whom He had promised."

So then, it is to all the children of adoption, to all those who are the brethren of Jesus by sanctifying grace that the Holy Spirit is given. And because this Gift is Divine and contains every most precious gift of life and of holiness, His effusion in us—an effusion which was manifested with such abundance of the first Pentecost— "fills the whole world with overflowing joy."[13]

---

[7] Versicle of the *Alleluia* of the Mass.   [8] Sequence *Veni Sancte Spiritus*.
[9] Hymn *Veni Creator*.   [10] Sequence *Lauda Sion*.
[11] Hymn *Veni Creator*.   [12] Galatians 4:6.
[13] Preface of Pentecost.

11.   The Holy Spirit vivifies the Church

THE Holy Spirit is the agent of all sanctification in the Church. The supernatural activity of the children of God in its different degrees depends on His vivifying influence. "For whoever are lead by the Spirit of God, they are the sons of God."[1] This is our faith.

It is incumbent on all to establish as perfect a harmony as possible between their personal spirituality and their faith. Let us consider, therefore, whether we allow the Holy Spirit to play a sufficient part in our interior life. Are we convinced of the absolute necessity for our sanctification of exposing our soul fully to His salutary influence?

It is beyond doubt that Jesus came into the world to reveal the Father. "Father . . . I have manifested Thy Name to the men whom thou has given me out of this world."[2] But, in the divine economy, this was not the sole object of His coming. It was ordained, also, that man should learn from the sacred lips of the Saviour to know the Holy Spirit and to venerate Him as the equal of the Father and the Son.

Hence, this astonishing saying of Jesus to His disciples, "It is expedient for you that I go." What does this mean? Christ came to save us, to guide us, to be everything to us, and now He declares that it is expedient that He should go. The reason given by Our Lord is still more astonishing. "If I do not go, the Advocate will not come to you."[3] Had we been present, we would perhaps have replied, "Master, we have no need of the Paraclete; You are sufficient for us. Stay with us and do not send a substitute." And yet Jesus declares clearly, "It is expedient for you that I go."

According to the designs of the Father, it is by faith that the children of adoption must enter into contact with the supernatural world: with Christ, the Church, the sacraments and, above all, with the Eucharist. It is by faith that they must hope in God, love Him, and serve Him. This doctrine supposes the disappearance of the visible Jesus from among us, and the invisible but vivifying influence of the Holy Spirit. It is for Him to guide the Church and each individual soul to its eternal destiny.

Christ the ideal of the Priest, chapter XVI, section 1.
[1] Romans 8:14.   [2] John 17:6.   [3] John 16:7.

The mission of the Holy Spirit is revealed to us by the gospel as being ordained to complete the work of Christ. When Jesus had pronounced the *consummatum est* on Calvary, what evidence had we of the efficacy of His precious blood to sanctify us? Jesus had preached certainly; He had trained His apostles; He had given them their first holy communion a few hours earlier; He had ordained them priests. Yet with the Passion of the Lord everything seemed lost; the disciples were terror-stricken; Peter denied his Master.

But at Pentecost, the disciples were filled with the Holy Spirit and the face of the world was renewed.[4] Peter no longer fears anyone. He appears in the middle of Jerusalem and preaches Christ.

The voice of the twelve is borne to the ends of the world, and in a few years the Christians are numbered in thousands. How has this prodigy been brought about? We find the answer summed up in the Preface for the feast of Pentecost. " Christ . . . ascending over all the heavens and sitting at the right hand of the Father, according to His word, sent down the Holy Spirit upon the children of His adoption."

From this moment, the Church, in spite of the most bitter persecutions, in spite of doctrinal disputes, and even the faithlessness of her own children at times, has lived and triumphed in a wondrous manner. She advances through the centuries, strong in her prerogatives which are the unmistakable marks of her divine institution. She is always one in her faith and in her allegiance to the successor of St. Peter. At all times she produces sanctity in her members by virtue of her own sanctifying power. She includes, as of right, the whole human race in her fold.[5] Finally, based on the foundation of the apostles, she remains indefectible.

The Church, one, holy, catholic, apostolic, and Roman is at the same time divine and of this world. She is assailed and surrounded by perils, but she holds out and advances, always unchanged in her divine constitution, indefectible in her faith, and continuously vivified by the Holy Spirit. Even the repeated renewal and reform within the human element of the Church is guided by this Divine Spirit.

What do we know about this Holy Spirit? Let us raise our eyes to the Holy Trinity.

The Son, begotten from all eternity, is the image of the Father, as we acknowledge everytime we recite the *Credo*: " God of God, light

[4] Psalm 103:30.   [5] Matthew 28:19-20.

of light . . ." But He is reflected back into the bosom of the Father and this union of the Father and the Son is fruitful. Proceeding from the unique breath of their mutual love, the Holy Spirit is infinite love and refers Himself entirely, as such, to His principle of origin.

Sanctity consists in dedicating oneself to God in charity. The third Person of the Blessed Trinity, because He is entirely oriented to the Father and the Son by an eternal reflection of love, is supremely worthy to be called "holy". The Holy Spirit is His proper name.

The Holy Spirit, proceeding from the love of the Father and the Son is, furthermore, the infinite gift which seals their union. He is the consummation, the final achievement, of the communication of the life in God.

As the gift of love in the bosom of the Trinity, He is for us the supreme gift of the Almighty—"The Gift of God most high!" With the Church, and in the same sense as she does, we venerate in Him the guest of our souls. He dwells in them and makes of them temples of the Lord. "For holy is the temple of God, and this temple you are."[6]

The Holy Spirit descends upon the whole Church and upon each Christian with all the riches of grace; "Living fountain, flame, love!"[7] He is the life-giving fountain of supernatural inspiration, the fire which gives ardour, the charity from which springs the sactification of souls and the union of hearts.

Coming to us, He brings His gifts. The liturgy recognizes seven; this number is traditional in the Church. It signifies the plenitude of the operation of the Holy Spirit in our souls.

The gifts are accessory to the state of grace. They are infused permanent dispositions, distinct from virtues and conferring on the Christian a special aptitude for receiving light and impulses from on high. By this influence of the Holy Spirit, it becomes possible for the children of God to act under the movement of a superior instinct and in a manner which excels the rational exercise which is normal for the virtues.

The exercise of these gifts establishes the Christian in an atmosphere which is entirely supernatural. In this way, the resemblance to the Son of God is perfected in him in the most exalted manner.

Although this cannot be accomplished without supernatural inspiration, our acts of faith, hope and charity, as well as our acts of

[6] I Cor. 3:17.   [7] Hymn *Veni Creator Spiritus*.

the infused moral virtues are exercised by us according to the rational procedure proper to all the superior activity of man; we move ourselves to act by weighing the motives and reasons. On the other hand, when a man acts by virtue of the gifts of the Holy Spirit, the sentiments which he experiences and the acts which he exercises are the product of a divine impulse. While not opposed to reason, they are not determined by it. The psychological process is supra-discursive; it is the outcome of a superior divine motion and is carried out in a manner which theologians call superhuman, or divine.

In practice, the activities of the virtues and the gifts are interwoven, and the more closely the soul is united to Christ, the more it is subject to the influences of the Holy Spirit. This fact stands out in the lives of the saints.

God places in us, with charity, these virtues, and the gifts of the Holy Spirit. All this ensemble of grace finds its consummation in the fruits of the Holy Spirit. These appear in the soul when the habits of a holy life reach their maturity; they manifest the harmonious and perfect development of the different virtues now in their flood. Outstanding among these are peace and spiritual joy, condescension and meekness..

This supernatural development is human in its expressions, but divine in its origin. From within, grace exalts nature and its activities. We must always see Jesus Christ as the source of this divine life, poured out in the Church and in each individual soul in the Church, through the operations of the Holy Spirit.

12. The Sacrament of Divine Adoption

BAPTISM is the sacrament of divine adoption.

By divine adoption we become children of God. Baptism is like the spiritual birth by which the life of grace is conferred upon us.

We possess within us, first of all, the natural life, the life we receive from our parents according to the flesh. By it, we enter into the human family; this life lasts some years and then ends in death. If we had only this natural life, we should never behold the Face of

Christ the Life of the Soul, part 2, chapter II, section 1.

God. It makes us children of Adam, and, by that very fact, stained from our conception with original sin.

Issued from Adam's race, we have received a life poisoned at its source. We share in the disgrace of the head of our race. We are born, says St. Paul, " children of wrath. St. Augustine puts it more drama- tically, " Whenever someone is born, Adam is born, the condemned from the condemned."[1] This natural life, which plunges its roots in sin, is of itself sterile for heaven. " The flesh profits nothing."[2]

But this natural life, born of man, born of the will of the flesh,[3] is not the only one. God, as I have said, wills to give us a higher life which, without destroying the natural life in so far as it is good, surpasses it, upraises and deifies it. God wills to communicate His own life to us.

We receive this Divine life through a new birth, a spiritual birth by which we are born of God.[4] This life is a participation in the life of God. It is, of its nature, immortal. " For you have been reborn," says St. Peter, " not from corruptible seed but from incorruptible, through the word of God who lives and abide forever."[5] If we possess this life here below we have the pledge of eternal beatitude, we become the heirs of God. If we have it not, we are forever excluded from the Divine fellowship.

Now, the regular means, instituted by Christ, whereby we are to be born to this life, is Baptism.

You know that episode related by St. John[6] of the interview of Nicodemus with Our Lord. This doctor of the Jewish law and member of the great council comes to find Jesus, doubtless so as to become His disciple, for he regards Christ as a prophet. Our Lord replies to his question, " Amen, Amen I say to thee, unless a man be born again, he cannot see the kingdom of God." Nicodemus, not understanding, asks Christ, " How can a man be born when he is old? "

What does Our Lord reply? What he had already said, but explaining it, " Amen, Amen I say to thee, unless a man be born again of water and the Spirit, he cannot enter into the kingdom of God." To be baptized, that is to say, to be plunged into water in order to be purified, was something very well known to the Jews. It only remained to be explained to them that there was to be a Baptism

---

[1] St. Augustine, Enarr. in Ps. 132.   [2] John 6:64.   [3] John 1:13.
[4] John 1:13.   [5] 1 Peter 1:23.   [6] John 3:1-21.

D

in which the Holy Spirit, uniting Himself to the water, would renew the spirit of man.[7] So Our Lord next contrasts the two lives, the natural and the supernatural. "That which is born of the flesh is flesh, and that which is born of the Spirit is spirit." And He concludes anew, "Do not wonder that I say to thee, 'You must be born again.'"

The Church at the Council of Trent[8] determined the interpretation of this passage, applying it to Baptism: The water regenerates the soul by the virtue of the Holy Spirit. The ablution of the water, sensible element, and the effusion of the Spirit, divine element, join to produce the supernatural birth. This is what St. Paul has already said, "But when the goodness and kindness of God our Saviour appeared, then not by reason of good works that we did ourselves, but according to his mercy, he saved us through the bath of regeneration and renewal by the Holy Spirit; whom he has abundantly poured out upon us through Jesus Christ our Saviour, in order that, justified by his grace, we may be heirs in the hope of life everlasting."[9]

Thus, you see, Baptism constitutes the Sacrament of adoption. Plunged in the sacred waters, we are there born to the Divine life. That is why St. Paul calls one who is baptized "a new man."[10] God, in making us partakers of His nature in so liberal a manner, by a gift infinitely exceeding all we could hope or expect, creates us, so to speak, anew. We are—it is still the great Apostle's expression—"a new creature;"[11] and because this life is Divine, it is the whole Trinity who makes this gift to us.

At the beginning of time, the Trinity also presided over the creation of man, "Let us make man to our own image and likeness."[12] It is also in the name of the Father and of the Son and of the Holy Spirit that our new birth is wrought. It is however, as the words of Jesus and St. Paul denote, especially attributed to the Holy Spirit, because it is especially through love that God adopts us. "Behold what manner of love the Father has bestowed upon us, that we should be called children of God; and such we are."[13]

Stress is laid on this thought in the prayers for Holy Saturday when the Bishop blesses the baptismal waters to be used in the sacrament.

---

[7] Bossuet, *Meditations upon the Gospel*, 36th day.

[8] Session 8 *De Baptismo*, canon 2.   [9] Titus 3:5-7   [10] Ephes. 3:15; 4:24.

[11] 2 Cor. 5:17; Gal. 6:15.   [12] Genesis 1:26.   [13] 1 John 3:1.

Listen to some of these prayers; they are very full of significance.

"O Almighty and Eternal God . . . send forth the Spirit of adoption to regenerate the new people whom the font of Baptism brings forth . . ." " Look down, O Lord, on Thy Church and multiply in her Thy new generations." Then the Bishop calls upon the Divine Spirit to sanctify these waters, "May the Holy Spirit vouchsafe by a secret impression of His Divinity to render fruitful this water for the regeneration of men: to the end that those who are sanctified in the immaculate womb of this sacred font, and born again new creatures, may come forth a heavenly offspring."

All the mysterious rites which the Church multiplies at this moment, all the invocations of this magnificent benediction replete with symbolism, are full of this thought—that it is the Holy Spirit who sanctifies the waters in order that those who are plunged in them may be born to the divine life, after having been purified from all sin: " so that all who receive this sacrament of regeneration may be born again, new children of perfect innocence."

Such is the greatness of this Sacrament. It is the efficacious sign of our Divine adoption. By Baptism we truly become the children of God and are incorporated with Christ. It opens the door to every heavenly gift.

Remember this truth: all God's mercies towards us, all His condescension, proceed from our adoption. When we turn the gaze of our soul towards the Godhead, the first thing that is unveiled to us of the eternal counsels regarding us, is the decree of our adoption in Jesus Christ. All the favours God may shower down upon our souls here below, until the day when He communicates Himself to us forever in the beatitude of His Trinity, have for their first link this initial grace of Baptism, to which they are attached.

At this predestinated moment,[14] we entered into the family of God; we became members of a Divine race, assured in principle of an eternal inheritance. At the hour of our baptism, Christ engraves an indelible character upon our soul; we receive the pledge of the Divine Spirit[14] which renders us worthy of the complacency of the Eternal Father, and assures us, if we are faithful to preserve this pledge, of all the favours God gives to those whom He regards as His children.

That is why the Saints, who have such clear insight into super-

---

[14] Ephes. 1:4-6; Romans 8:29.

natural realities, have always held baptismal grace in most high esteem. The day of Baptism was for us the dawn of Divine liberality and future glory.

13. The Indwelling Spirit

I F the visible and extraordinary character of the effects of the work-ings of the Holy Spirit have in great part disappeared, the action of this Divine Spirit ever continues in souls and it is not the less wonder-ful for now being chiefly interior.

Holiness for us is nothing else that the complete unfolding, the full development of that first grace of our divine adoption, that grace given at baptism by which we become children of God and brethren of Christ Jesus. The substance of all holiness is to draw from this initial grace of adoption all the treasures and graces which it con-tains and that God causes to flow from it. Christ is the model of our divine filiation. He has moreover merited that it should be given to us, and He Himself has established the means whereby it should come to us.

But the fruition within us of this grace, rendered possible by Jesus, is the work of the Holy Trinity. It is however, and not without motive, especially attributed to the Holy Spirit. Why is this? Always for the same reason. This grace of adoption is purely gratuitous and has its source in love. " Behold what manner of love the Father has bestowed upon us, that we should be called children of God; and such we are."[1] Now in the adorable Trinity, the Holy Spirit is sub-stantial love. St. Paul tells us that, " the charity of God " (that is to say the grace that makes us children of God) " is poured forth in our hearts by the Holy Spirit who has been given to us."[2]

And from the moment of the infusion of grace in us by baptism, the Holy Spirit abides in us with the Father and the Son. " If any-one love me, he will keep my word, and my Father will love him, and we will come and make our abode with him."[3] Grace makes our soul the temple of the Holy Trinity. Our souls, adorned with grace are truly the abode of God; He dwells within us, not merely as He

Christ the Life of the Soul, chapter VI, section 4.   [1] John 3:1.
[2] Romans 5:5.   [3] John 14:23.

does in all things, by His essence and His power, by which He sustains and preserves every creature in existence, but in an altogether special and intimate manner as being the object of supernatural knowledge and love.

And because grace thus unites us to God, because it is the principle and measure of our charity, it is especially the Holy Spirit who is said "to dwell within us," not in a manner that is personal to Him to the exclusion of the Father and the Son, but because He proceeds through love and it is He who unites the Father and the Son. "He will dwell with you and be in you," says Our Lord.[4] Every man, even a sinner, still possess in himself the vestiges of divine power and wisdom; the just alone, those who are in a state of grace, are partakers of the supernatural charity which is like the exclusive sign of the Holy Spirit. This is why St. Paul, speaking to the faithful, says to them, "Or do you not know that your members are the temple of the Holy Spirit, who is in you, whom you have from God."[5]

And what is it this Divine Spirit does in our souls? For being God, being Love, He does not remain inactive. First of all, He gives testimony that we are the children of God. "The Spirit himself gives testimony to our spirit that we are sons of God."[6] He is the Spirit of Love, the Spirit of Holiness, whose will it is, because He loves us, to give us a share in His holiness that we may be true and worthy children of God.

With sanctifying grace which, so to speak, defies our nature and renders it capable of acting supernaturally, the Holy Spirit places within us forces, "habits," which raise the faculties of the soul to the divine level. These are the supernatural virtues, above all the theological virtues of faith, hope and charity, which are, properly speaking, the virtues characteristic of our state as children of God. Next there are the infused moral virtues which help us in the combat against the obstacles that are opposed to the development of the divine life within us.

Lastly, there are the gifts of the Holy Spirit. Let us take a few moments to consider them. Our Divine Saviour, who is our model, received them, as we have seen elsewhere, but in a transcendent and eminent manner. The measure of the gifts in us is limited; however this measure still remains so fruitful that it produces marvels of holi-

[4] John 14:17.   [5] 1 Cor. 6:19.   [6] Romans 8:16.

ness in souls where these gifts abound. Why is this? Because it is chiefly by them that our state of adoption is especially brought to perfection as we are about to see.

What then are the gifts of the Holy Spirit? They are benefits, as the name indicates, that the Spirit gratuitously distributes to us with sanctifying grace and the infused virtues. In her liturgy, the Church tells us that the Holy Spirit is Himself the highest Gift[7] for He descends into us even from the moment of baptism to give Himself as the object of love. But this gift is divine and living. He is a Guest who, full of liberality, wishes to enrich the soul that receives Him. Being Himself the uncreated Gift, He is the source of the created gifts which, with sanctifying grace and the infused virtues, fully enable the soul to live supernaturally in a perfect manner.

Indeed, even supplied with grace and the infused virtues, our soul is not re-established in that original integrity in which Adam was before the fall. Reason, itself subject to error, sees its power of sovereignty disputed by the inferior appetites and the senses; the will is prone to weakness.

What follows from this state? It follows that in the principal work of our sanctification, we are under the necessity of being constantly and directly aided by the Holy Spirit. He provided for this by His inspirations which all go to perfect, to achieve our sanctity. And in order that these inspirations may be well received, He himself places in our souls the dispositions that render us docile and pliable. These are the gifts of the Holy Spirit.[8]

The gifts therefore are not of themselves inspirations of the Holy Spirit, but dispositions which cause us to obey these inspirations promptly and easily.

By these gifts, the soul is made capable of being moved and directed in the path of supernatural perfection and of divine filiation. It possesses, as it were, a supernatural tact, a divine instinct of supernatural things. The soul that, in virtue of these dispositions, lets itself be guided by the Spirit, acts in all security as becomes a child of God. In all its spiritual life, it thinks and acts " supernaturally to

[7] Hymn *Veni Creator*.

[8] In Christ Jesus the presence of the gifts of the Holy Spirit does not proceed from the necessity of aiding the weakness of the reason and will, Christ not being subject to any error or weakness. These gifts were bestowed upon the soul of Jesus because they constitute a perfection and it is befitting that every perfection should be in Christ.

the point " if I may thus express myself.[9] You will at once see that
the gifts place and dispose the soul to move in an atmosphere where
all is supernatural, where nothing natural, so to speak, is mingled.
By His gifts, the Holy Spirit holds and reserves to Himself the
supreme direction of all our supernatural conduct.

And this is a most important point for us, our holiness being of an
essentially supernatural order. By the virtues, the soul in a state of
grace acts supernaturally, it is true; but it acts in a manner conform-
able to its rational and human condition as likewise by its own movement and initiative. By the gifts it is disposed to act directly and
solely under the divine impulsion (while keeping, of course, its
liberty which is manifested by acquiescence to the inspiration from
on high), and this in a manner which does not always fit in with its
national, natural way of seeing and considering things.

The influence of the gifts is then, in a very real sense, superior to
that of the virtues.[10] It is true that the gifts do not supply the place
of the virtues but they marvellously complete their operations. For
example, the gifts of understanding and knowledge perfect the exercise of the virtue of faith. This explains why souls, simple and
uncultured, but upright and docile to the inspirations of the Holy
Spirit, have a certitude, a comprehension of supernatural things and
a penetration into them that is sometimes astonishing. They have a
spiritual instinct which warns them of error and makes them hold
to the revealed truth with a singular assurance protecting them from
all doubts. Whence does this arrive? From study? From deep
examination into the truths of their faith? No, from the Holy Spirit,
the Spirit of Truth who by the gift of understanding or of knowledge perfects their virtue of faith.

As you see, the gifts constitute for the soul a perfection of great
value on account of their exclusively supernatural character. They
achieve the bringing to perfection of that wonderful supernatural
organism by which God calls our souls to live by the Divine life.
Granted to every soul in a state of grace, in a greater or lesser
measure, the gifts remain in a permanent state as long as we do not
drive out, by mortal sin, the Divine Guest who is their source.

As it is always possible for them to increase, they moreover extend
to all our supernatural life which they make extremely fruitful

[9] St. Thomas, *Summa* 1a 2ae, q.68, a.3.
[10] St. Thomas, *Sentences* 3, dist. 34, q.1, a.1; and dist. 35, q.2, a.3.

because by them our souls are placed under the direct action or immediate influence of the Holy Spirit. Now the Holy Spirit is God with the Father and the Son; He loves us with unspeakable love; He wills our sanctification; His inspirations, all proceeding from His goodness and love, have no other end than to mould us to a greater resemblance to Jesus. And this is why, although it is not their proper and exclusive function, the gifts even dispose us to those heroic acts by which holiness is powerfully manifested.[11]

What ineffable goodness is that of our God who supplies us so carefully and richly with all that is necessary for us in order to attain Him! And would it not be doing a wrong to the Divine Guest of our souls if we were to doubt His goodness and love, to fail in confidence in His bounty and liberality or show ourselves heedless about profiting by them?

14.   The Gifts of the Holy Spirit

LET us now say a word on each of the seven gifts. This number does not constitute a limit, for the action of God is infinite, but rather, like many other biblical numbers, it denotes plenitude. We will simply follow the order indicated by Isaias in his Messianic prophecy without seeking to establish a gradation or any carefully marked characteristics in the relations between the gifts; we will try to say, as far as we can, what belongs to each of them.

The first mentioned is that of *wisdom*. What does wisdom signify here? It is a supernatural gift whereby we know or esteem Divine things by the spiritual taste with which the Holy Spirit inspires us. It is an intimate, a deep knowledge that relishes the things of God. We ask for it in the collect for the feast of Pentecost itself, " Grant us to be ever truly wise . . ." To be " wise " here, is to have not only the knowledge, but the relish for celestial and supernatural things. It is not, far from it, what is called sensible devotion, but a spiritual experience of what is Divine, that the Holy Spirit wills to produce within us.

Christ the Life of the Soul, chapter VI, section 5.
[11] Graham, Dom Aelred, *The Love of God*, N.Y., Longmans, Green, 1940. Section 2, chapter 2.

It is the response to the Psalmist's invitation, "Taste and see that the Lord is sweet."[1] This gift makes us prefer, without any hesitation, the blessedness of God's service to all earthly joys. It is this gift which causes the soul to say, "How lovely are Thy tabernacles, O Lord! Better is one day in Thy courts above thousands,"[2] of years away from God! But to experience this, we must carefully put away all that draws us towards the unlawful pleasures of the senses.

The gift of *understanding* makes us search deeply into the truths of the faith. St. Paul tells us that, "God has revealed them through his Spirit. For the Spirit searches all things, even the deep things of God."[3] Not that this gift diminishes the incomprehensibility of the mysteries or does away with faith. But it goes further into the mystery than the simple acquiescence of faith. It bears upon the appropriateness or the greatness of the mysteries, upon their relations with other or with our supernatural life.

It has also for its object, the truths contained in the sacred books, and it is this gift which seems to have been granted in a special measure to those in the Church who have shone by the depth of their doctrine, those whom we call "Doctors of the Church."

Every baptised soul possesses within itself this precious gift. You read a text of Holy Scripture; you have read and reread it many times without having been struck by it. Then, one day, a sudden light flashes, illuminating to its depth, so to speak, the truth set forth in this text. This truth then becomes altogether clear to you and often a principle of supernatural life and action. Is it by your reflections that you have arrived at this result? No, it is an illumination, an intuition of the Holy Spirit who, by the gift of understanding, makes you penetrate further into the inmost and deep meaning of the revealed truths so that you may hold them the more firmly.

By the gift of *counsel,* the Holy Spirit responds to this prayer of the soul, "Lord, what wilt Thou have me to do?"[4] He keeps us from all precitation, from all levity, but above all, from all presumption, so dangerous in spiritual ways. A soul that only wishes to be guided by itself, who worships its own personality, acts without consulting God. That soul, practically, acts as if God were not for it the heavenly Father from whom every light comes. "Every good

---

[1] Psalm 33:9.
[2] Psalm 83:2-11.
[3] I Cor. 2:10.
[4] Acts 9:6.

gift and every perfect gift is from above, coming down from the Father of Lights."[5]

Consider our Divine Saviour. He says the Son, that is to say Himself, does nothing " but only what He sees the Father doing."[6] The soul of Jesus contemplated the Father beholding in Him the model of His works. It was the Spirit of Counsel that showed Him the desires of the Father; that is why all that our Lord did was pleasing to His Father. " I do always the things that are pleasing to Him."[7] It is a disposition whereby the child of God is enabled to judge of things according to principles above those of human wisdom. Sometimes, natural prudence, always limited, points out how to act in such or such a way; then, by the gift of counsel, the Holy Spirit shows higher principles of conduct which ought to direct the actions of the child of God.

It is not always enough for us to know God's good pleasure. Owing to our fallen nature, we often need strength to carry into effect what God requires of us; it is the Holy Spirit who, by the gift of *fortitude,* sustains us in particularly difficult moments. There are pusillanimous souls that fear the trials of the inner life. It is impossible that these trials should be wanting; they are even so much the deeper in proportion as God calls us higher.

But let us fear nothing: the Spirit of Fortitude is with us. " He will dwell with you and be in you."[8] Like the Apostles on the day of Pentecost, we shall be, by the Holy Spirit, endowed with power from on high so as to accomplish the Divine will generously, to obey, like the Apostles, God rather than men, if the choice must be made;[9] to support valiantly the adversities we meet with as we come nearer to God.

That is why St. Paul prayed so earnestly for the faithful of Ephesus that God would grant them " to be strengthened with power through his Spirit unto the progress of the inner man."[10] The Holy Spirit says to such as He fills with fortitude, what God said to Moses when he shrank from the mission given to him of delivering the Hebrew people from the yoke of the Pharaohs: fear nothing for " I will be with thee."[11] Such a one is strong with the very strength of God. It is this strength that makes the martyrs and sustains the

[5] James 1:17.   [6] John 5:19.   [7] John 8:29.
[8] John 14:17.   [9] Acts 4:19.   [10] Ephes. 3:16.
[11] Exodus. 3:12.

virgins. The world wonders to see them so courageous because it imagines they find their strength in themselves, while in reality they draw it from God alone.

The gift of *knowledge* makes us see created things in a supernatural way as only a child of God can see them. There are many ways of considering what lies within and around us. It is in a different manner that an unbeliever and one who believes in God contemplate creation. The unbeliever has only a purely natural knowledge, however wide and profound it may be; the child of God sees creation in the light of the Holy Spirit, as the work of God wherein His eternal perfections are reflected.

This gift makes us know created things, including ourselves, from God's point of view. It makes us know our supernatural end and the means of arriving at it, but with intuitions which preserve us from the false maxims of the world and the suggestions of the spirit of darkness.

The gifts of piety and of fear are the complement, the one of the other. The gift of *piety* is one of the most precious because it concurs directly in regulating the attitude we ought to keep in our relations with God: the blending of adoration, respect and profound reverence towards the Divine Majesty; of love, confidence, tenderness, perfect abandonment and holy liberty in the presence of Him who is our heavenly Father.

Far from excluding each other, these dispositions can be perfectly allied; but it is the Holy Spirit who will teach us in what measure they are to be harmonized. In the same way, love and justice do not exclude one another in God. The gift of piety bears another fruit: it reassures timid souls (there are such) who in dealing with God are afraid of not employing the right formulae in their prayers. This scruple is dispelled by the Holy Spirit when one listens to His inspirations. He is the "Spirit of Truth." If, says St. Paul, "We do not know what we should pray for as we ought,"[12] the Spirit is within us to help us. He prays in an ineffable manner which makes us cry towards God and be heard by Him.

Lastly there is the gift of *fear of the Lord*. It seems strange, does it not, to find the prophet Isaias use the expression "He shall be filled with the Spirit of fear." How can this be? How can Christ, the Son of God, be filled with the fear of God? It is because there are two

[12] Romans 8:26.

kinds of fear of God. First, there is the fear which thinks only of
the chastisement due to sin; that is servile fear, wanting in nobility
but not always without use. Then there is the fear which makes us
avoid sin because it offends God; that is filial fear but it remains
imperfect as long as the fear of punishment is mingled with it. It
goes without saying that neither this imperfect fear nor servile fear
had any place in Christ's all-holy soul.

There was only perfect, reverential fear, the fear that the angelic
powers have before the infinite perfection of God,[13] the fear that
shows itself by adoration and is altogether holy. "The fear of the
Lord is holy and remains for ever and ever."[14] If we could contemplate the humanity of Jesus, we should see it prostrate in reverence
before the Word to Whom His humanity is united. This is the reverence that the Spirit places within our souls. He keeps it there but in
mingling it, by the gift of piety, with that love and filial tenderness
which results from our Divine adoption and makes us cry out to
God: "Father!" This gift of piety implants in us, as in Jesus, the
tendency to refer everything to our Father.

Such are the gifts of the Divine Spirit. They perfect the virtues by
disposing us to act with a supernatural assurance which constitutes
in us, as I have said, what is like a Divine instinct of heavenly things.
By these gifts, which the Holy Spirit places within us to render us
docile to His action, He achieves the work of making us more and
more the children of God. "For whoever are led by the Spirit of
God, they are the sons of God."[15]

When therefore we let ourselves be guided by the promptings of
this Spirit of Love; when we are, in the measure of our weakness,
constantly faithful to His holy inspirations—those inspirations that
lead us towards God and what is pleasing to Him—the result is that
we act in the full meaning of our Divine adoption. Then our souls
produce those fruits which are at once the term of the Holy Spirit's
action in us and, by their sweetness, are like the anticipated reward
of our fidelity to this action.

These fruits, as enumerated by St. Paul, are charity, joy, peace,
patience, benignity, goodness, longanimity, mildness, faith, modesty,
continence and chastity.[16] These fruits, all worthy of the Spirit of
love and holiness, are also worthy of our heavenly Father who finds

[13] Preface of the Mass.   [14] Psalm 18:10.
[15] Romans 8:14.   [16] Galatians 5:22-23.

glory in them. "In this is my Father glorified, that you may bear very much fruit."[17] Finally, they are worthy of Christ Jesus who merited them for us and to whom the Holy Spirit unites us. "He who abides in me, and I in him, he bears much fruit."[18]

The Holy Spirit, whom Christ, as the Word, sends us, is within us the principle, the source of those rivers of living waters, of the grace which springs up within us into life everlasting[19] that is to say, that makes us bear fruits of everlasting life. While awaiting the supreme beatitude, these waters "make joyful the city" of souls.[20] St. Paul says, too, that all faithful souls, those who believe in Christ have all been given to drink "of one Spirit."[21] That is why the liturgy, the echo of the teaching of Jesus and of the Apostles, causes us to invoke the Holy Spirit who is also the Spirit of Jesus, as the "Living Fountain."[22]

15. The Gifts of Fear, of Piety and of Fortitude

RIGHT through our life, in every action of our spiritual activity, we must invoke the sanctifying intervention of the Holy Spirit. Let us consider more attentively His activity in the most sublime moment of our daily life: our Holy Mass.

It is in all truth a very great honour for us to be associated with and participate in the sacrifice of Jesus Christ in His priestly act. It is the Holy Spirit alone who can give us that inner elevation of soul to fit us for such a function.

Speaking of the oblation of Christ on Calvary, St. Paul is careful to note that it was carried out under the influence of the Holy Spirit. "Who through the Holy Spirit offered Himself unblemished unto God."[1] Let it be the same for us. Let us offer this unique sacrifice with our souls adapted to receive the impulse of the Spirit of Love.

I would like to suggest to you how the Holy Spirit can exercise a

---

[17] John 15:8.   [18] John 15:5.   [19] Cf. St. Thomas *In Joanne* 7.
[20] Psalm 45:5.   [21] 1 Cor. 12:13.   [22] Hymn *Veni Creator*.
Christ ideal of the Priest, chapter XVI, section 4 (adapted).
[1] Hebrews 9:14.

most salutary influence on us by means of His gifts while we are at
Mass. I would like to call your attention, by a brief outline, to the
riches of grace which they bring to us.

The gifts of fear and piety have special significance for the celebration of, and the participation in, the holy sacrifice of the Mass. It is
their part to inspire the most fundamental attitudes of soul at this
sacred moment. We must never forget at the altar the immense,
fathomless, infinite majesty of the most holy God to whom the sacrifice is offered.

As creatures, we must stand before God in an attitude of adoration
and self-effacement under the pain of failing in truth, and it is at
Mass especially that we must be possessed by these sentiments. The
Mass is essentially an act of worship which acknowledges the absolute
rights of God, an act of homage to His supreme sovereignty. Christ
offered His sacrifice on the Cross in that spirit of intimate reverence
and religious respect towards the Father which was fitting in the
pontiff as well as in the victim of so sacred an act. When we approach
so close to the divinity, we must make these sentiments of the heart
of Jesus our own.

Let us conceive also, like the Saviour, a keen aversion for all the
sins of the world, for all the offences against the supreme Goodness,
and let us foster in our soul the eager desire to make reparation for
them.

Through the secret impulse of the Holy Spirit attributable to the
gift of piety, we will come to appreciate that the spirit in which the
sacrifice is offered must be one of filial love. By what name does the
liturgy address the Lord? By the name of Father. And our access to
the divine majesty is free, assured, and confident. So intimate is our
communion with the Father that we can venture to associate ourselves with His loving delight in His Son and to share in it. The
priest at the altar identifies himself with Jesus; how fully then must
this filial spirit be manifest in him!

Let us ask the Holy Spirit to inspire us with a lively faith in God's
love for us and with absolute confidence in our heavenly Father.

Under the influence of the divine Spirit, we shall feel ourselves
impelled at Mass to take upon ourselves all the needs of the human
race for, by the gift of piety, we are associated interiorly with the
charity which filled the heart of Jesus Christ. As we consider the
many sorrows of this world, we shall think of the sinners for whom

Christ shed His blood. We shall think of the afflicted, the sick, the dying, and in the face of this immense chorus of unhappiness which rises from this vale of tears, we shall implore the divine mercy for all. Or rather, it is Christ who will ask His Father to have pity on them.

Jesus has willed to assume all our infirmities.[2] When we offer Jesus to His heavenly Father, it is Jesus Himself, clothed, as it were, in all the ills of His members, who implores divine clemency. These dispositions of piety are perfectly consistent with reverential fear, as one of the liturgical prayers asserts so admirably: "Bestow on us, O Lord, both an abiding fear and an abiding love of Thy holy Name."[3]

Instead of approaching the holy sacrifice with a cold heart we can enkindle it with these burning truths. Then the Holy Spirit will inspire us and make us pray with more fervour.

The gift of fortitude is necessary on account of the great faith required. The very formula of consecration reminds us that this is "the mystery of faith." It is this same gift which gives us the courage to offer ourselves each day to God as victims dedicated to all the desires of His will, even the most crucifying. When our cross seems too heavy to accept or bear, let us ask the Holy Spirit to inspire us with something of the supernatural fortitude which filled Jesus at the moment of His sacrifice.

16. The Gifts of knowledge, understanding and counsel

We come now to the three intellectual gifts of knowledge, understanding and counsel. You must not be confused by the fact that I have changed the customary order. When we are at Mass, the important thing is not so much to know whether the Lord is directing us by this gift or that, as to have an active faith in the influence from on high and a soul fully disposed to receive them.

You may be quite sure that the most sublime ideas about the Mass will be quite incapable of bringing us close to God unless they are

Christ the ideal of the Priest, chapter XVI, section 5 (adapted).
[2] Isaiah 53:4.　　　　[3] Collect, 2nd Sunday after Pentecot.

illuminated by the Holy Spirit. It is an excellent thing, certainly, to know one's theology and especially all that it teaches about the holy sacrifice, but you might read the most learned writings on the subject and yet feel as cold and uninspired as before. Why? Because it is the brain that has done all the work. We must have a supernatural sense of the divine mysteries to complement our studies. There must be something to complete the letter of our reading. Now, it is only the Holy Spirit of love who can give us a deep, living knowledge of the eucharistic offering and immolation.

By the gift of knowledge, the Holy Spirit inspires in us a supernatural appreciation of created things, that is to say, He makes us judge of their importance or unimportance according to the judgement of God. Scripture calls this kind of knowledge the knowledge of holy things.[1] By virtue of this higher rectitude of judgement, the saints emancipated themselves from the fascination of the world and exclaimed with St. Paul, "I count everything loss because of the excelling knowledge of Jesus Christ, my Lord. For his sake I have suffered the loss of all things, and I count them as dung that I may gain Christ."[2]

This gift enables us also to understand the incomparable value of the realities of faith and of sacred acts of worship. That is why we should implore the Holy Spirit to give us a true understanding of the value of the Mass in accordance with the outlook of God Himself on the august sacrifice.

This understanding will not be the fruit of reasoning. It is intuitive, but the intimate conviction which it gives us is most fruitful.

May the Holy Spirit graciously grant us the grace in silence and prayer to appreciate, as God appreciates them, the mysteries which are renewed each day in the holy sacrifice of the Mass.

By the gift of understanding, the Holy Spirit casts light on the truths of faith in themselves in the depths of our souls. "For the Spirit searches all things," says St. Paul, "even the deep things of God;" it is He also who makes us know " the things that have been given us by God."[3]

In our ordinary life, when we read something, our understanding, by its own light, extracts the meaning which the words express. This is why St. Thomas writes, "To understand is to read inside."[4]

[1] Wisdom 10:10.   [2] Philippians 3:8.
[3] 1 Cor. 2:10-12.   [4] St. Thomas Summa 2a 2ae q 8, a.1.

Something analogous occurs in the supernatural order. A secret light enables our soul to enter in some small measure into the truth which God illuminates. It is true certainly that the Christian already accepted this truth by a simple act of faith. He held it as true but as something outside himself. By the gift of understanding the truth is fully revealed.

The Church affirms the reality of these interior lights in many of her prayers. "May the Spirit, O Lord, who proceeds from thee enlighten our understanding and may He, even as Thy Son has promised, lead us into all truth."[5] In this way, we enter, in a certain manner, into the very sanctuary of the divinity.

You will readily understand the value of this gift for those who offer the holy sacrifice or participate in it. A divine act is accomplished on the altar; neither man nor angels can grasp the full significance of it, or measure its amplitude. It is ineffable. The Son of God is there. He offers Himself. He immolates Himself under the sacred species. He gives Himself. The Father looks on the son . . .

It is only a ray of light from on high that can enable us to understand something of the mysteries and to adapt our souls to them. When we read the texts of Holy Scripture and the liturgy, we must have faith that for us, as for the disciples after the Resurrection, the Holy Spirit can make clear their sense. "Then He opened their minds, that they might understand the Scriptures."[6] These sacred words conserved religiously in our hearts will become more and more soul-stirring to awaken in us the love of God.

The gift of counsel disposes us to recognize, as though by a superior instinct, what actions are useful to guide us and others to our supernatural destiny. "For whoever are led by the Spirit of God, they are the sons of God," says St. Paul.[7] By virtue of this gift, in the ordinary course of life, the Holy Spirit protects us from the impulsiveness of our nature, from our pride, from our self-opinionatedness. These defects are sources of illusion and of error in the spiritual domain. They incline us to act without giving due consideration to the views of God on the individual souls.

The gift of counsel does not seem to have any great part to play in the celebration of the holy sacrifice. Yet, the Mass is the supreme moment to ask for those lights of which we stand in such great need.

[5] Collect of Wednesday of Pentecost Week.   [6] Luke 24:45.
[7] Romans 8:14.

E

How indispensable these lights are to us in our words, in our deci-
sions, in all the activities of our vocations and our daily duties of
state!

Still, it is important to realize that our faith in the intervention of
the Holy Spirit does not justify us, in the carrying out of our duties,
in neglecting wise judgement and human means. The gift of counsel
was not given by God to His children to replace the virtue of prudence, but, on the contrary to assist it and perfect its activity.[8]

[8] St. Thomas, *Summa*, 2a 2ae q.52, a.2.

17. The Gift of wisdom

T H E most eminent of the gifts is wisdom. It is a knowledge of God
and of things divine gained in the actual exercise of the life of union
with the Lord. This wisdom is a fruit of charity; it is therefore of
quite another order to theoretic or reasoned knowledge. It is sweet;
it establishes an intimate living contact between the soul and God.

How are these things possible? They are possible through the
secret action of the Holy Spirit. When the Christian prays and serves
God with great fidelity and love, the Holy Spirit gives him this
supernatural wisdom while his soul is concentrated on the Lord.
The soul savours the presence of God. It experiences in a certain
manner, in its inner being, His merciful goodness and the communication of His life which He makes to the children of adoption.

By this gift, the Holy Spirit inspires the human heart to prefer
unhesitatingly the beatitude of union with God to all the joys of this
world and to say with the Psalmist, "How lovely are Thy tabernacles, O Lord! Far better is one day in Thy courts above thousands."[1] However, we can only dispose ourselves to enjoy this
spiritual savour if we put out of our life the desires and indulgences
of the world. "The sensual man does not perceive the things that
are of the Spirit of God,"[2] says St. Paul.

In holy Mass, we get quite a different understanding of the eucharistic mysteries from that given by a reasoned study. A supernatural
attraction establishes in our hearts the true spirit of oblation.

Christ the ideal of the Priest, chapter XVI, section 6.
[1] Psalm 83:2, 11.   [2] I Cor. 2:14.

Besides, have we not immense need of divine help to enable us to savour the eucharistic bread spiritually? We frequently repeat the phrase, "Bread from heaven . . . containing all happiness"[3] and yet, when we are about to receive Holy Communion, it may happen that we feel no sensible desire for this Bread of life.

The gift of wisdom produces also in the heart an inner peace which supports the soul in the midst of the difficulties and sorrows of life. This is why the liturgy likes to see in the Holy Spirit the supreme consoler; frequently the Church makes us ask that we may at all times enjoy His consolations. How desirable is this peace, coming from God! Thanks to it, during the Holy Sacrifice of the Mass, we will feel in the depths of our hearts the effects of the eternal goodness.

Incomplete as this outline is, it may serve to enlighten and enliven our faith and our hope in the action of the Holy Spirit, especially during the sacred mysteries, and thus help us overcome the spirit of routine.

Before Mass, we can draw inspiration from that prayer of the Missal: "May Thy good Spirit enter into my heart; there in silence to cry aloud to me; there to give wordless utterance to all truth. For exceeding deep are the secrets of God and over them He has cast a sacred veil."[4]

Liturgical tradition proclaims the faith of the Church in the intervention of the Holy Spirit during the sacrifice of the Mass. Without entering into the problem of the ancient formulas of the *epiklesis,* we may consider the prayers of the offertory as we have them today. When the bread and wine have been prepared on the Altar, the congregation is offered in union with it. What does the priest do then? He raises his hands over the whole oblation and invokes the coming of the Holy Spirit: "Come Thou Sanctifier, almighty, eternal God!"

We may consider the ceremony of the consecration of an altar, one of the most ancient ceremonies in the liturgy. After the table of sacrifice has been purified by aspersions and consecrated by anointings, they place on the five crosses, which represent the five wounds of Jesus, grains of incense which are burnt, and, as the incense burns, the pontiff with his clergy sends up to heaven the prayer, *Veni Sancte Spiritus.*

It is one of the most solemn moments in this great ceremony.

[3] Versicle and Response at Benediction.   [4] Preparation for Mass: Sunday.

They implore by the Holy Spirit, the flame of love, to come down on to this altar where Jesus is to offer Himself, through the Holy Spirit, as He did on the Cross. They ask Him to sanctify all the oblations that will be placed upon it and, above all, by the fullness of the power of Holy Communion to unite the holocaust of the whole Christian assembly to the divine Victim.

By the sacraments of baptism, confirmation, and holy orders we receive a permanent character in our souls, uniting us to Christ the High Priest and forming in us a share in His own Priesthood. We receive the Holy Spirit in a very special way through these sacraments. His mission in us is invisible, but by it, we are assured of heavenly aid through the whole course of our life. Let us honour the Holy Spirit equally with the Father and the Son by a worship of adoration, by a homage of profound gratitude and of total abandonment to God's will, and by constant fidelity to His inspirations. In this manner, we shall be led to serve God as St. Paul recommends "with the joy of the Holy Spirit."[5]

CONSECRATION OF THE HOLY TRINITY: O Eternal Father, prostrate in humble adoration at Thy feet, we consecrate our whole being to the glory of Thy Son, Jesus, the Word Incarnate. Thou hast established Him as King of our souls; submit to Him our souls, our hearts, our bodies; let nothing in us move except by His orders, except by His inspiration.

United with Him may we be borne into Thy bosom and consummated in the unity of Thy love. O Jesus, unite us to Thee in Thy life of perfect sanctity, wholly consecrated to Thy Father and to souls. Be unto us our wisdom, our justice, our sanctification, our redemption, our *all*. Sanctify us in truth.

O Holy Spirit, love of the Father and the Son, establish Thyself as a furnace of love in the centre of our hearts and bear constantly upwards, like eager flames, our thoughts, our affections, and our actions even to the bosom of the Father. May our entire life be a *Gloria Patri et Filio et Spiritui Sancto*.

O Mary, Mother of Christ, Mother of fair love, do thou form us according to the heart of Thy Son.

---

[5] I Thessalonians I:6.

This act of consecration, the climax of a period of generous fidelity, became the point of departure for new and great spiritual progress. It is dated Christmas, 1908.

18. The Holy Spirit and the Priest

HEAVEN has its oblation, eminent and ineffable, continuous and altogether glorious. The Incarnate Word did not will to leave the earth without likewise bequeathing to it a sacrifice. This sacrifice is the Holy Mass which both recalls and reproduces, in a mystical manner, the immolation of Golgotha.

The sacrifice of the Cross is the one and only sacrifice. It suffices for all, but Our Lord willed that it should be renewed in order to apply the fruit of it to souls. Let us contemplate the sublime mystery of the extension of Christ's priesthood and see how Our High Priest perpetuates His sacrifice here below.

Christ chooses certain men to whom He gives a real participation in His Priesthood. These are the priests whom the bishop anoints on the day of their ordination. Extending his hands over the head of the one whom he is about to consecrate, the bishop invokes the Holy Spirit, beseeching Him to descend upon that soul. At that moment the word that the angel spoke to Mary might be repeated to the priest. " The Holy Spirit shall come upon thee."[1]

The Holy Spirit envelops him, as it were, and effects within him so close a union and resemblance with Christ Jesus that he is, like Christ, a priest for all eternity. Christian tradition calls the priest " another Christ": he is, like Him, chosen to be, in the name of Christ, a mediator between heaven and earth. This is a supernatural reality. When the priest offers the Sacrifice of the Mass, which reproduces the Sacrifice of Calvary, he is identified with Christ. He does not say " This is Christ's Body; this is Christ's blood;" if he said this, there would not be sacrifice. But he says, " This is My Body; this is My Blood."

From the moment of ordination, the priest consecrated to God by the Holy Spirit becomes, like Christ, a pontiff and mediator between men and God. Or rather, it is Christ's one mediation prolonged here below through the ages, by the ministry of priests. In the name of the faithful, the priest offers to God the Eucharistic Sacrifice upon the altar; from the altar he brings to the people the Holy Victim, the Bread of Life, and therewith, every gift and every grace.

Christ in His mysteries, chapter V, section 5.   [1] Luke 1:35.

The altar is, on earth, the centre of the religion of Jesus, as Calvary is the summit of His life. All the mysteries of the terrestial existence of Jesus converge, as I have said elsewhere, towards His immolation upon the Cross. From the Cross all the states of His glorious life derive their splendour.

That is why the Church does not commemorate nor celebrate any of the mysteries of Jesus without offering the Holy Sacrifice of the Mass. All the public worship organized by the Church gravitates around the altar. All the lessons, prayers, praises, readings and homage known as the Divine Office, and in which the Church exalts the mysteries of her Divine Bridegroom and retraces them under the eyes of her children, were regulated by her only so as to enshrine the Eucharistic Sacrifice.

Whatever then be the mystery of Jesus that we celebrate, the best way to participate in it and to dispose ourselves to make the fruit of it our own is, after having mediated upon it and contemplated it, to assist with faith and love at the Holy Sacrifice of the Mass and to unite ourselves, by Holy Communion, to the Divine Victim, immolated for us upon the altar.

In the life of Blessed Mary d'Oignies, it is related that Our Lord was accustomed, on the occasion of the different feasts, to show Himself to her in the Blessed Sacrament under a form in harmony with the mystery being celebrated.[2]

We have no need to envy this favour. By Holy Communion, Christ Jesus does not only show Himself to the soul; He comes within us, He communicates Himself entirely to us. He comes with His humanity as a compassionate High Priest, knowing our frailty, and with the virtue of His divinity which is able to raise us up to Himself at His Father's right hand. He comes within us in order to pray to the Father in us, with us; to offer Him Divine homage and unite thereto our supplications; but above all to bring forth in our innermost souls, by His Spirit, the fruit of each of His mysteries.

You will have noticed that the thanksgiving which follows the holy Oblation and Communion (postcommunion) takes a different aspect according to the different mysteries. What does this indicate if not that by Holy Communion, Christ wishes to make arise within us the thoughts and sentiments that He experienced when living the mystery that is being celebrated that day, and consequently wishes

[2] Father Faber, *The Blessed Sacrament.*

to apply to us the special fruits and graces proper to this mystery. Thus the Holy Spirit, through the ministry of the ordained priest, effects the work of Christ-likeness in our souls.

This is what the Church asks at the postcommunion on the feast of the Holy Rosary, wherein she honours the Mother of the Incarnate Word as united with all the mysteries of her Son, Jesus. What does the Church ask of God in the collect of the Mass? In her prayer to God, she brings forward the plea that " His only-begotten Son has, by His life, death, and Resurrection merited for us the reward of eternal life." Then she asks, " that in honouring these mysteries, we may imitate what they contain and obtain what they promise. A like thought inspires the " postcommunion " of the feast: " Grant, O Lord, that we may obtain the virtues of the mysteries we celebrate."

Thus, little by little, our identification with Jesus is realized. " Have this mind in you which was also in Christ Jesus."[3] Is not that the very formula of our eternal predestination? " To become conformed to the image of His Son."[4]

The Eternal Word—made flesh for us—becomes, by His mysteries and His Sacrifice, our High Priest and our Mediator. A Mediator who knows our needs, because He has been a man like unto us; and an all-powerful Mediator, because He is God with the Father and the Holy Spirit; a Mediator whose mediation is unceasing, in heaven by His eternal oblation, and on earth by the Eucharistic Sacrifice.

And it is for us that Christ accomplishes this work. Christ saves us by His Sacrifice only in order to associate us with His glory. And the instrument He uses to join us to His Sacrifice is the priest, set apart from men for the things that pertain to God,[5] when the ordaining Bishop calls down the power of the Holy Spirit to effect so wonderful a transformation.

O Lord, who shall be able to reveal how ineffable are the designs of Thy wisdom? Who shall celebrate the greatness of the gift Thou dost make to us? Who shall be able to render Thee thanksgiving worthy of it!

[3] Philippians 2:5.
[4] Romans 8:29.
[5] Hebrews 5:1.

19. The Holy Spirit and the Liturgy

Pope St. Pius X wrote. "The active participation of the faithful in the sacred mysteries and in the public and solemn prayer of the Church is the first and indispensable source of the Christian Spirit."[1]

It is then true to say that when we contemplate Christ's different mysteries in their successive order in the liturgical cycle, we do so not only in order to evoke the remembrance of events wrought for our salvation, and to glorify God for them by our praise and thanksgiving. It is not only to see how Jesus lived and strive to imitate Him, but even more, that our souls may participate in each special state of the Sacred Humanity and draw forth from it the proper grace that the Divine Master attached to it in meriting this grace as Head of the Church for His Mystical Body.

On this subject there is, in fact, a truth of great importance too often forgotten or even sometimes unknown.

Man can imitate Christ, our Model, in two ways. He can strive to imitate Him by purely natural efforts, as when one aims at reproducing a human ideal presented by some hero or other personage whom one loves or admires. There are people who think it is in this manner that we must imitate our Lord and reproduce in ourselves the traits of His adorable person.

This is to lose sight of the truth that Christ is a divine model. His human beauty and virtues, His manliness, have their roots in His Divinity and from it they derive all their splendour. We can, and assuredly must, with the help of grace, make every effort to comprehend Christ and to model all our virtues and actions upon His. But, the Holy Spirit alone is capable of reproducing within us the true image of the Son, because our imitation must be of a supernatural order.

Now this work of the Divine Artist, the Spirit of Jesus, is wrought above all in prayer based upon faith and enkindled by love. While, with the eyes of faith and the love that yearns to give itself, we contemplate Christ's mysteries, the Holy Spirit, who is the Spirit of Jesus Christ, acts within our inmost soul and fashions it, by His

Christ in His mysteries, excerpts from Chapter II, section 2, and chapter VI, section 3.

[1] Pius X, *Motu Proprio*, 23 Nov. 1903.

sovereignly efficacious touches, in such a way as to reproduce within it, as by a sacramental virtue, the traits of the Divine Model.

This is why the contemplation of the mysteries of Jesus is so fruitful in itself. This is why the essentially supernatural contact with the states of her Spouse, into which the Church, guided by the Holy Spirit, places us in the liturgy is so vital for us. There is no surer way nor more infallible means for making us one with Christ.

For Christ did not come only for the inhabitants of Judea, His contemporaries. He came to give life and light to all of us, to men of every nation and century. Do we not sing in the *Credo* ". . . He came down from heaven for us and for our salvation . . ."? The "fullness of time" is not yet ended; it will endure as long as there shall be souls to save.

But it is the Church of Christ, since His Ascension, that Our Lord has commissioned to bring Him forth in souls. "My dear children," said St. Paul, the Apostle of Christ Jesus among the nations, "with whom I am in labour again, until Christ is formed in you."[2] The Church, guided by the Holy Spirit, labours at this work by making us contemplate every year the mysteries of her Divine Bridegroom.

All Christ's mysteries are living mysteries; they are not merely historical realities of which we recall the remembrance, but the celebration of each mystery brings a proper grace, a special virtue intended to make us share in the life and states of Christ whose members we are.

The Holy Spirit, who governs the Church and is the first author of our sanctification, wills that each year we strive to enter into the interior dispositions of Christ through the cycle of liturgical mysteries and feasts. Following Christ Jesus in this manner in all His mysteries, uniting ourselves to Him, we share, little by little, but surely, and each time more fully and deeply, in His divinity and in His divine life. According to the beautiful words of St. Augustine, that which was formerly brought to pass in a divine reality, is spiritually received in fervent souls by the repeated celebration of these mysteries.[3]

[2] Galatians 4:19.
[3] St. Augustine, Sermon 220, on the vigil of Easter.

20. The Holy Spirit and Prayer

W H A T is prayer?

We will define it as the intercourse of the child of God with his heavenly Father. You will note the words "the intercourse of the child of God." I have used them designedly. Sometimes men are to be met with who do not believe in Christ's divinity, like certain deists of the eighteenth century and such as those who instituted, at the French Revolution, the cultus of the Supreme Being and invented prayers to the "Divinity." They perhaps thought to dazzle God with these prayers which were nothing better than the vain conceits of a purely human spirit that God could not accept.

Such is not our prayer. It is not simply as creatures we speak with God, but as children with our heavenly Father, coming before Him to adore and praise Him, to tell Him of our love, to learn to know His will and to obtain from Him the necessary help to accomplish this will.

Undoubtedly, we can never forget our condition of creatures, that is to say, of nothingness, but the point of departure, or rather the stand-point on which we ought to place our intercourse with God is the supernatural stand-point. In other words, it is our Divine sonship, our quality of children of God through the grace of Christ, that ought to determine our fundamental attitude in prayer.

Hear how St. Paul throws light on this point. " But in like manner the Spirit also helps our weakness. For we do not know what we should pray for as we ought, but the Spirit himself pleads for us with unutterable groanings."[1] Now St. Paul says, in the same place, this Spirit who prays for us and in us, is the Spirit of adoption that " gives testimony to our spirit that we are sons of God. But if we are sons, we are heirs, also . . . by virtue of which we cry, ' Abba, Father '."[2]

This Spirit was given to us when " the fullness of time came, God sent His Son, born of a woman . . . that we might receive the adoption of sons."[3] Because the grace of Christ makes us the children of God, He has also sent the Spirit of his Son into our hearts so that we may pray to God as to a Father. " And because you are sons, God

Christ the Life of the Soul, part 2, chapter X, section 1.   [1] Romans 8:26.
[2] Romans 8:15-17.   [3] Gal. 4:4-5.

has sent the Spirit of His Son into our hearts . . ."[4] Because, indeed, we are no longer strangers and foreigners but members of God's family, built upon the foundation of which Christ Jesus is the chief corner-stone.[5]

Let us listen to Our Lord Himself. He came to be the "Light of the world," and His words, full of truth, tell us the way we are to follow. "I am the Way and the Truth and the Life."[6]

Seated upon the edge of Jacob's well, He speaks with the Samaritan woman.[7] This woman has just acknowledged that He who speaks to her is a prophet, one sent by God, and at once she asks Him (it was the subject of lively debate between her compatriots and the Jews) if God must be adored on the mountains of Samaria or at Jerusalem.

And what does Christ reply? "Woman, believe me, the hour is coming when neither on this mountain nor in Jerusalem will you worship the Father. . . . But the hour is coming and is now here, when the true worshippers will worship the Father in spirit and in truth. For the Father also seeks such to worship Him." At Samaria, as you know, false gods were adorned, and that is why Christ says it is "in truth," that is to say it is the true God who must be adored. At Jerusalem, the true God was adored, but not "in spirit;" the religion of the Jews was altogether material in its expression and in its aim.

Note how Our Lord lays stress on the name of Father. It is the incarnate Word who inaugurates (the time "is now here") the new religion, that of the true God, adored in spirit, the spirit of the Divine, supernatural, and spiritual adoption, whereby we are made children of God. That is why Our Lord is so insistent on this term "Father."

The true adorers shall adore the Father in spirit and truth. Doubtless, as we are adoptive children, and as God, while making us His children, diminishes nothing of His Divine majesty nor of His absolute sovereignty, we must adore Him, prostrate ourselves before Him. But, it is in spirit and in truth that we must adore Him; that is to say in the truth and spirit of the supernatural order whereby we are His children.

Our Lord is elsewhere still more explicit. With the Samaritan

---

[4] Gal. 4:6; cf. Rom. 8:15; 2 Cor. 1:22.   [5] Ephes. 2:20.
[6] John 8:12; 14:6.   [7] John 4:5-45.

woman He has, so to speak, laid down the principle. With His disciples He gives the example. One day, says St. Luke, He was praying, and "when he ceased, one of his disciples said to him, 'Lord, teach us to pray.'"[8]

What reply does Christ give? "When you pray, say 'Our Father who art in heaven, hallowed be thy name . . ." Never forget this: Our Lord is God. As the Word, He is ever in the bosom of the Father; no one knows God except the Son. Christ, then, knows perfectly what we ought to say to God, or ask Him, so as to be those "true adorers" for whom God seeks. He knows perfectly, too, in what attitude we ought to come before God in order to speak with Him and be pleasing to Him.

He reveals to us that which He sees. "The only-begotten Son, who is in the bosom of the Father, he has revealed him."[9] And we must listen to what He reveals. He is the Way we must follow without fear; he who follows this way "does not walk in darkness."[10] Now what does Jesus say when He wants to teach us this science of prayer that He has declared to be so necessary that we ought always to pray?[11] He begins by pointing out the title we ought to give to God before offering Him our homage, this title that is like the direction, or, if you will, the tone that is to be given to the conversation, and on which we are to support our petitions—the title that denotes what the attitude of our soul should be in God's presence. And what is this title? "Our Father . . ."

We thus gather from the very lips of Christ, the beloved Son in whom the Father is well-pleased, this precious teaching that the first and fundamental disposition we must have in our relations with God is that of a child in the presence of his father. Certainly, once more—and this point is not less important—this child will never forget his primitive condition of a creature fallen in sin and having within him a source of sin that is able to separate him from God: for He who is our Father dwells in heaven and is likewise our God.

"I ascend to my Father and to your Father, to my God and to your God,"[12] said Our Lord when about to leave his apostles. That is why the child of God will always have deep reverence and great humility; he will pray that his sins may be forgiven, that he may not succumb to temptation, that he may be delivered from evil; but he

---

[8] Luke 11:1-13; Matthew 6:9-13.   [9] John 1:18.   [10] John 8:12.
[11] Luke 18:1.   [12] John 20:17.

will crown this humility and this reverence with unshaken confidence—for "every good gift and every perfect gift is from above, coming down from the Father of Lights,"[13]—and with a tender love of a son for his father, and for a father who loves him.

Prayer, then, is like the expression of our intimate life as children of God, like the outcome of our Divine sonship in Christ, the spontaneous blossoming of the gifts of the Holy Spirit. And that is why it is so vital and so fruitful. The soul that gives itself regularly to prayer derives from it ineffable graces that transform it little by little to the image of Jesus, the only Son of the heavenly Father. St. Teresa says, "the door by which graces of choice, such as those God has given me, enter into the soul, is prayer; once this door is closed, I do not know how He could grant them to us."[14]

The soul, too, derives from prayer a joy resembling a foretaste of the blissful union of heaven, of that eternal heritage awaiting us. "Amen, amen I say to you, if you ask the Father anything in my name, he will give it to you . . . that your joy may be full."[15]

Such is mental prayer: a heart to heart communing between God and the soul, "a communing alone with God, so as to express our love to Him by whom we know ourselves to be loved."[16]

And this communing of the child of God with his heavenly Father is accomplished under the action of the Holy Spirit.

God promised by the prophet Zacharias, that, under the new covenant, He would pour out upon souls the spirit of grace and of prayers.[17] This spirit is the Holy Spirit, the Spirit of adoption, whom God sends into the hearts of those whom He predestines to be his children in Christ Jesus. The gifts which this Divine Spirit confers on our souls on the day of baptism, by the infusion of grace, help us in our relations with our Father in heaven.[18]

The gift of fear fills us with reverence in the presence of the Divine Majesty. The gift of piety harmonizes, with fear, the tenderness of a child towards a beloved father. The gift of knowledge places the truths of the natural order in a new light. The gift of understanding makes us penetrate into the hidden depths of the mysteries of faith.

---

[13] James 1:17.   [14] St. Teresa. *Life by herself*, chapter 8.   [15] John 16:24.
[16] St. Teresa, *Life by herself*, chapter 8.   [17] Zach. 12:10.
[18] Among recent writers who treat of the nature of prayer under the action of the Holy Spirit, note: Leen: *Progress through mental prayer*; and Boylan: *This tremendous lover*.

The gift of wisdom gives us the relish, the affective knowledge of revealed truths. The gifts of the Holy Spirit are very real dispositions which we do not take enough into account. It is by these gifts that the Spirit, who dwells in the soul of the baptised as in a temple, helps and guides us in our intercourse with the heavenly Father. "The Spirit himself helps our weakness (and) pleads for us with unutterable groanings."[19] "The Holy Spirit is the very soul of our prayers. He inspires them and makes them always acceptable."[20]

The essential element of prayer is the supernatural contact of the soul with God whence it imbibes that Divine life that is the source of all holiness. This contact is produced when the soul, raised by faith and love, supported by Jesus Christ, yields itself to God, to his will, through the movement of the Holy Spirit. The wise man "will give his heart to rise early to the Lord who made him, and he will pray in the sight of the Most High."[21] No reasoning, no purely natural effort, can produce this contact. "No one can say 'Jesus is Lord' except in the Holy Spirit."[22] This contact is produced in the darkness of faith, but it fills the soul with light and life.[23]

Prayer is, then, the expression, under the action of the gifts of the Holy Spirit, of the sentiments that result from our Divine adoption in Jesus Christ, and that is why it is accessible to every baptised soul of good will. Moreover, Christ Jesus invites all His disciples to tend to perfection so that they may be worthy children of the heavenly Father. "You therefore are to be perfect, even as your heavenly Father is perfect."[24]

Now perfection is only practically possible if the soul lives by prayer. Is it not therefore evident that Christ has not willed that the manner of treating with Him in prayer should be difficult or beyond the capacity of the most simple souls that sincerely seek Him? This is why I have said that mental prayer may be defined as the intercourse or conversation of a child of God with his heavenly Father. "In this manner therefore shall you pray: Our Father who art in heaven."[25]

---

[19] Romans 8:26.
[20] Catechism of the Council of Trent, part 4, chapter 1, section 7.
[21] Eccli. 39:6.
[22] 1 Cor. 12:3.
[23] This is a favourite theme in the works of Fr. Thomas Merton.
[24] Matthew 5:48.
[25] Matthew 6:9.

21. Preparation for prayer

PRAYER is the intercourse of the child of God with his heavenly Father; thereby we adore Him, praise Him, tell Him our love for Him, learn to know Him and His will, and obtain from Him the necessary help for the perfect accomplishment of this will. Prayer is the normal outcome, under the Holy Spirit's action, of the affections resulting from our divine adoption.

This definition affords us a glimpse of the primary qualities which prayer ought to have. If prayer be the conversations of the child of God with his heavenly Father, it will bear the impress both of a high degree of piety and of a deep reverence.

Indeed, for the child of God, for the brother of Christ Jesus, no tenderness, no intimacy is too great, but on the condition that it be always accompanied and sustained by a sense of unutterable reverence before the immense majesty of the Father. This is to adore the Father in spirit and in truth.[1]

And it is this double character that St. Benedict requires in his Rule. What does he tell us, in fact, in that chapter on the reverence we ought to have at prayer? He would have us first of all offer our supplications to the Lord God of all things with all lowliness and purity of devotion: that is the note of reverence.

We are to draw near to God with that sense of respect before His infinite perfections, which is expressed by a humble attitude and the longing to be pure in the presence of holiness itself.

St. Benedict wishes our prayer to be " pure and short," unless, he adds—and here comes in the note of submission of heart proper to an adopted child of God—"unless it be perchance prolonged by the inspiration of Divine grace."[2]

The Holy Patriarch requires then that we come before God with respect and humility, as befits creatures, and creatures who have sinned. But this deep reverence which holds us prostrate before Him in all submission, does not prevent the heart from opening out, under the movement of the Holy Spirit, in confidence, love, and tenderness. This confidence is so much the surer in that it rests exclusively on the goodness of our Father in heaven.

Christ the ideal of the monk. Chapter XV, section 2 and passim.
[1] Cf. John 4:23.　　　　　[2] St. Benedict. *Holy Rule*, chapter 20.

In the prologue to his holy Rule, St. Benedict recalls these divine words:[3] "My eyes will be upon you, and My ears will be open to your prayers, and before you call upon Me, I will say unto you: 'Behold I am here!'" What can be sweeter, the great Patriarch immediately adds, than this voice of the Lord inviting us and showing us the way of life?

Thus appears the double aspect of piety as St. Benedict understands it. These affections are both necessary; they are inseparable, as our condition of creatures and our character of children of God are inseparable. If an unrestrained familiarity, forgetful of reverence, is perilous, fear, separated from confidence, is not less so. Each of these two attitudes is a wrong done to God: irreverence, to His infinite sovereignty: servile fear, to His boundless goodness.

The reverence and this confidence are possible and are maintained only if we take care to prepare ourselves for our communication with God. Some might say: Since it is the Spirit of Jesus who prays within us, we can come into God's presence without preparation. To think in this way would be to make a great mistake. We cannot expect the Holy Spirit's action to be forthcoming in our souls independently of certain interior conditions.

"The Spirit himself pleads for us,"[4] says St. Paul, but the same apostle warns us not to "grieve"[5] nor "extinguish"[6] the Spirit. Now, how do we extinguish the Spirit? By mortal sin, which forces Him to separate Himself from the soul. How do we grieve Him? Certainly not by the frailities that we deplore, the faults that take us by surprise, but we grieve Him by our infidelities and our deliberate resistance to divine inspirations.

We must, then, if we would make the life of prayer possible, and prayer itself fruitful, watch over the purity of our heart. St. Benedict holds much to this quality. It is "the purity of our devotion" he says, which is to be the condition of our supplications. The soul that does not strive to purify itself of its faults by compunction, to avoid as far as possible all that could be displeasing to God, cannot attain to a life of union with Him through prayer. It wilfully grieves the Holy Spirit who must uphold the soul in prayer. It is in this purity that the preparation of the heart consists, a remote preparation, but always necessary.

[3] Cf. Psalm 33:16; Isaiah 65:24; 58:9.   [4] Romans 8:26.
[5] Ephesians 4:30.   [6] I Thessalonians 5:19.

Another preparation, of a more intellectual character, is likewise demanded. The Holy Spirit guides us according to our nature: intellect and will. Before entering into prayer, we ought to possess some knowledge of the things of faith which will serve us as elements for this communing with God.

You may say that God sometimes gives a soul the gift of prayer even before it has acquired great knowledge of the mysteries of faith and dogma, or is completely purified. Undoubtedly this is so, but it is not the general way. We here find a certain analogy between the manner in which God governs the natural world and His mode of action in the order of grace.

See how things come to pass in the order of creation. God could produce effects without the concourse of secondary causes; He could create bread and wine without man having to sow and reap, plant and gather the grapes. Did He not change water into wine at Cana? And multiply the loaves in the desert? He is the sovereign Master of all the elements, but His glory requires that the habitual course of things be ruled by the laws which His eternal wisdom has established. God will that the vine shall be planted and the leaves bud forth, that the fruit shall ripen and be gathered by man and go through the wine-press, before the wine is poured into the cup.

After the same manner in the supernatural order, there are laws fixed by divine wisdom and shown by the experience of the Saints. Undoubtedly, God is not enslaved by His laws. Thus, He makes certain souls pass in an instant from the state of sin to a state of perfect love. Magdalen, by the disorders of her life, was at the anti-thesis of love; it needs but a word from Our Lord to change her life into one of glowing beauty.

Again, look at Saul. He is a persecutor of the Christians, breathing out threats and persecutions,[7] hating the disciples of Jesus and blaspheming the Christ. He is overthrown on the road to Damascus and our divine Saviour makes of him, in an instant, a vessel of election, an apostle full of fire, who preaches Christ from whom nothing can henceforth separate him. In the same way, we read in the life of St. Teresa that in one of her Carmels, a novice received the gift of prayer without anything having prepared her for this grace.

But, these are exceptional gifts or extraordinary prodigies in which God manifests His sovereign power, and reminds us of the infinite

[7] Acts 9:1-15.

F

liberty of His Spirit, and of His Spirit's action. God's ordinary way of leading souls to Himself is to have respect for the laws of which He is the Author.

God has not left us the treasures of revealed faith for us to keep them buried, as if they were not worth the trouble of being studied or under the false humility that they are too sacred to examine, or we too ignorant to approach. The deposit of revelation was delivered to us in order that, with humility and with our eyes on the Church's teaching, we should exercise our intelligence in fathoming this deposit and in extracting from it all that is precious, glorious to God, and fruitful for our souls.

The lives of the saints show us that God loves this seeking after truth, the starting point of a more generous charity. When He wishes to lead to a higher degree of union a soul that is, naturally speaking, little instructed, like St. Catherine of Siena, He Himself will then take care of enlightening it by His Holy Spirit and of giving it in an infused manner the knowledge of the deepest mysteries, that it may find in them the secret of a more extensive love. Meanwhile, let us be persuaded that studying the truths of faith makes the "talent" confided to us, fructify, and we thus labour at our sanctification.

We shall find in the divine Office a pure and unfailing source of illumination, extremely fruitful for the inner life. When we are faithful in reciting the Divine Office *well,* the Holy Spirit, who inspired the Psalms and directs the Church in the organization of the worship of Jesus, gives us little by little a deep knowledge, full of unction and savour, of God's perfections and the mysteries of Christ; a knowledge more fruitful than any we could gain by study and reasoning. The Holy Spirit illumines with His divine light some truth, some word of mystery of Jesus. He deeply engraves them on the soul.

This knowledge, altogether heavenly, supernatural and sweet, fills the soul with humility and confidence, and thus illumined with divine splendours, it annihilates itself before God and surrenders itself entirely to His holy will. The Holy Spirit, as has been justly said, suggests the attitude of sincere souls, the inward attitude which places the soul before God in full truth.

For you will remark that the sacred texts are not taken from man. They come to us from heaven, and as none but the Holy Spirit who inspired them, can make us know their depth, so none but He alone, as Christ said, can make us understand the words that fell from the lips of the Incarnate Word, the actions accomplished, and the mysteries lived by the Saviour's sacred humanity. "He will teach you all things and bring to your mind whatever I have said to you."[8]

The Holy Spirit presents these truths in a divine light to our soul. They then become, as it were, the elements of our own life, without there being need of reasoning. The passing vividness of the first impression fades, it is true; but the truth has been deeply perceived and remains in the soul like a principle of life. "The words that I have spoken to you are spirit and life."[9]

The Divine Office is truly a granary prepared by God Himself, and those who recite it *devoutly* abound in the lights of the Holy Spirit. After a few years, prayer becomes an easy habit to them. Assiduous and daily acquaintance with the words inspired by God, is a sure and easy way of conversing with God.

"How can it be that a soul prepared and formed by the Holy Spirit should not know better than any other how to converse with God in the intimacy of the heart, returning as it does to its solitude, laden like a bee with honey from so many flowers. How can it be ignorant of the right words in which to address the Divine Majesty, when the soul enters into the secret chambers of its heart, all replenished with the Divine Word? What is contemplation in its highest form but the opening out of the beautiful affirmations which the prayer of the Church puts upon our lips? When a soul borrows expressions from human language, it will never find any words that more exactly convey the truths it has contemplated than the forms of liturgical prayer, lending themselves, as they do, with equal ease to the lispings of the soul beginning to seek God and to the enraptured outpourings of the soul that has found Him."[10]

Now, what better preparation for prayer can be found, what better way could be found of forming Jesus in us, than to contemplate His mysteries, and thereby obtain the strength to imitate them? The soul, faithful in following Christ step by step as the Church presents Him, infallibly arrives at reproducing within itself the character (in the deep meaning of the word) of Christ Jesus, and the ability of conversing intimately with Him. The Church in her liturgy is guided by the Holy Spirit, and it is this Spirit who not only

[8] John 14:26.   [9] John 6:64.

[10] Madame Cecile J. Bruyere, Abbess of Solesmes. *Spiritual Life and Prayer according to the Holy Scriptures and monastic tradition.*

enlightens us as to Christ's mysteries, but forms in us the features of Christ.

St. Paul tells us quite plainly that we cannot even pronounce the name of Jesus without the Holy Spirit.[11] With much greater reason, we are incapable, without the help of this Divine Artist, of reproducing in our souls the features of the heavenly Model, the form of our predestination and the Ideal of our perfection.

Undoubtedly we see souls succeed, by force of will and effort, in forming within themselves the human character, the natural virtues; but in order to form within us the Divine character, to engrave within us supernatural traits, the only ones that make us pleasing to God, it needs the action of the Holy Spirit, and this action is unceasing in the Liturgy.

Thus, a life of prayer which is like the continual echo of the liturgical life that each year makes us walk closer, by faith and reverence and love, in the steps of Christ Jesus, from the Incarnation to the Ascension, besides having a very sure and supernatural function, possesses incomparable efficacy and fruitfulness. The Holy Spirit will, indeed, be able to perfect the Christ-life in a soul which travels this path.

When a soul is thus faithful in following Christ Jesus step by step, in allowing itself to be replenished by the Holy Spirit with truths from on high and in conforming its life to them, God leads it little by little to the *state* of prayer. The third stage, that of the unitive life, is begun, where the soul clings solely to God, to Christ!

But solitude and silence must also be cultivated as a preparation for the life of prayer, the life of the spirit. Was it not in interior recollection that the Blessed Virgin lived? The gospel writes that she kept the word of her Divine Son in her heart, so that she might meditate upon them.[12] The Blessed Mother did not speak many words. Filled with grace and light from on high, inundated with the gifts of the Holy Spirit, she remained, silent, in the adoration of her Son. She lived on the contemplation of the ineffable mystery wrought in her and through her, and from the sanctuary of her immaculate heart a hymn of praise and thanksgiving rose up unceasingly to God.

God calls all baptized souls to be intimately united to Him. Are we not, by grace, His children, the brethren of the Son of His love, the living temples of His Holy Spirit? All the mysteries of Jesus, all

[11] I Corinthians 12:3.   [12] Luke 2.19.

the marvellous supernatural organism that He has established in His Church, to what do they tend, if not to open to upright, generous, and faithful souls, the way of love and most intimate union with Himself? " I have called you friends, because all the things that I have heard from my Father, I have made known to you."[13] Thus, Christ invites us to converse with Him in the intimacy of friendship, as the prelude to, and the result of, the formation of the Christ-life in us.

22. Prayer and Grace

IN a conversation, one both listens and speaks. The soul gives itself up to God, and God communicates Himself to the soul.

To be able to listen to God and receive His light, it is enough if the heart is filled with faith, reverence, humility, ardent confidence and generous love.

In order to speak to God, it is necessary to have something to say to Him. What is to be the subject of the conversation? That depends principally on two elements: the measure of grace that Christ Jesus gives to the soul, and the state of the soul itself.

The first element to be taken into account is the measure of the gifts communicated by Christ. " But to each one of us grace was given according to the measure of Christ's bestowal."[1] Christ Jesus, being God, is the absolute master of His gifts. He pours his light into us as it pleases his sovereign majesty. By this Spirit, Christ guides and draws us to his Father. If you read the masters of the spiritual life, you will see that they have always religiously respected the sovereignty of Christ in the dispensation of his favours and lights, and the freedom of the Spirit. That explains their extreme reserve when they have to intervene in the relations of the soul with God.

St. Benedict, who was a great contemplative, favoured with extraordinary graces of prayer, and was a past-master in the knowledge of souls, exhorts his disciples to give themselves frequently to prayer.[2] He makes it clearly understood that the life of prayer is absolutely

---

[13] John 15:15.
Christ the Life of the Soul, part 2, chapter X, section 2.
[1] Ephes. 4:7.   [2] St. Benedict, *Holy Rule*, chapter 4.

necessary in order to find God. But, when it concerns regulating the manner of giving one's self to it, he is singularly discreet. He naturally supposes one has already acquired a certain habitual knowledge of Divine things from the assiduous reading of the Holy Scriptures and the works of the Fathers of the Church.

Concerning prayer, he contents himself first of all with pointing out what ought to be the attitude of the soul when approaching God, namely, profound reverence and humility. It is remarkable that the great Patriarch of the West entitles the chapter on prayer in his Holy Rule, "Of Reverence at Prayer."[3] He wills that the souls should remain in God's presence in a spirit of great compunction and perfect simplicity. This is the best attitude in which to listen to the voice of God with profit.

As to mental prayer itself, beyond linking it closely with the psalmody (of which it is, as it were, only the interior prolongation), St. Benedict makes it consist of short and fervent aspirations of the heart towards God. Repeating the counsel of Christ,[4] he says we ought to avoid multiplicity of words. Our prayer ought to be short unless prolonged under the prompting of the Holy Spirit dwelling in the soul by grace. We do not find anything more formally laid down on this subject by the legislator of the monastic life.

Another great master of the spiritual life arrived at a high degree of contemplation, and full of the lights of grace and experience St. Ignatius Loyola wrote some words of which we cannot weight too much the deep wisdom. "For each one," he writes to St. Francis Borgia, "that meditation is the best in which God communicates Himself the most. For God knows and sees what is most suitable for us, and knowing all, He himself points out to us the way to be followed. But we first have to grope dimly, before finding this way which will lead us to the life that has no end where we shall enjoy the most holy gifts of God."[5]

St. Teresa of Avila, in different places in her writings, expresses the same thought: Whether a soul gives itself much or little to prayer, it is extremely important not to force it too much, nor to hold it back, as it were, chained in a corner.[6]

---

[3] St. Benedict, *Holy Rule*, chapter 20.

[4] Matthew 6:7.

[5] Quoted from *Etudes*, 1905, I., pp. 567-8.

[6] St. Teresa, *The Interior Castle*, First Mansion, chapter 2. Cf also her *Life*, chapters 12, 13, 18, and 27.

St. Francis de Sales is not less reserved. Hear what he says. The text is a little long, but it well characterizes the nature of prayer—the fruit of the gifts of the Holy Spirit—and the discretion necessary to regulate it.

"Do not suppose, my daughters, that prayer is a work of the human mind. It is a special gift of the Holy Spirit, raising the powers of the soul above natural strength, so that they may be united to God by sentiments and communications that all the discourses and wisdom of men cannot produce without Him. The ways by which He leads the saints in this exercise, (the most Divine employment of a reasonable creature), are wonderful in their diversity. And, they are all to be honoured, since it is to God they bring us, and they are under the guidance of God. But, we must not be anxious to follow them all, nor even to choose any of them on our own impulse. The important thing is to discover what is the attraction of grace for us and to be faithful to it."[7]

Such testimonies could be multiplied, but these are enough to show us that much as the masters of the spiritual life urge souls to give themselves to prayer—for it is a vital element of spiritual perfection—so, too, do they take care not to impose indiscriminately upon every soul one way rather than another. We say "impose." They praise or recommend certain ways; they suggest or propose particular methods; all have their value which it is well to know and all have their utility which can be experienced. But to wish to impose indifferently on every soul one exclusive method would be not to take into account either the Divine liberty with which Christ Jesus distributes his grace, nor the attractions placed in us by his Spirit.

As for the matter of method, what helps one soul might be a hindrance to another. Experience shows that many souls that have facility in speaking habitually and simply with God and gain much good from this intercourse, would be impeded if one tried to tie them down to such or such a method. It is then for each and every soul to study for itself first of all what is the best manner for it to converse with God.

Those generous souls who seek God should, on the one hand, consider their aptitudes, their dispositions, tastes, aspirations, and kind of life, and then seek to know the attraction of the Holy Spirit,

[7] St. Francis de Sales on "The Interior Life of the Nuns of the Visitation". (1744 ed.)

besides taking into account the progress they have made in spiritual ways. On the other hand, they should be generously docile to the grace of God and the action of the Holy Spirit. Once the best way is found, after some inevitable trials at the beginning, they should keep faithfully to it, until the Holy Spirit draws them into another way. This is, for them, the condition of gaining fruit from their prayer.

Another point I consider important, and one very closely allied with the preceding, is not to confound the essence of prayer with the methods, whatever these may be, that are used in making mental prayer. Some souls think that if they do not use such or such a method, they are not praying, a mistake which cannot be without danger in its consequences. Having bound up the essence of prayer with the use of some special method, they dare not change the method, even when they have recognized that it is an obstacle for them, or has become useless. Or even, which most often happens, finding the method wearisome, they relinquish it and, at the same time, relinquish the prayer itself, and this to their great detriment.

Method is one thing; prayer another. The method ought to vary according to the aptitudes and needs of souls, while prayer (I am speaking of ordinary prayer) remains substantially the same, always for every soul—an intercourse in which the child of God pours out his soul before the heavenly Father, and listens to Him, in order to please Him. The method, by sustaining the mind, helps the soul in its union with God. It is a means, but ought not to be, nor to become, an obstacle. If such a method enlightens the intelligence, warms the will, leads it to yield itself to the Divine guidance of the Holy Spirit, and to pour itself out before God, then it is good. But it should be abandoned when it really fetters the attraction of the soul, constrains us, and does not help us to make any progress in the spiritual way; or on the contrary, when it has become useless in consequence of the progress already made.

23. Union with God

WHILE our whole existence is dedicated to things holy and eternal, it must be passed amidst the vicissitudes of this earthly life. Under the influence of our environment there is a danger that we may live in too human a manner, and restrict ourselves to the mere material performance of the duties of our state in life, without rising to the supernatural significance of our vocations. Moreover, no matter how holy even sacred rites may be, repetition tends to introduce into them a certain routine by force of habit.

As a protection against this all-pervading naturalism and indifference, it is indispensable that the life-giving breath of the Holy Spirit should fructify each one of our actions. Only in this way can real, objective union with God be attained.

It is this Holy Spirit which will light in our hearts the flame of love. In spiritual matters it is He alone who gives full rectitude to judgement. He also it is who inspires the filial attitude which permits us in all truth to invoke the Lord as "Father". He it is who inspires our prayer: "The Spirit Himself pleads for us with unutterable groanings."[1]

These are some of the forms of the actions of the Holy Spirit in us. Whoever wishes to live as a child of God must try to keep his soul under this influence. How many know this Spirit of Love? And yet He alone is the source of their whole interior life. He alone fructifies all spiritual activity and effects our union with God.

How is an ecumenical council opened? By the hymn *Veni Creator*. If this is the rule for great official assemblies of the Church, let it be your rule also never to undertake any action of importance without first invoking the Holy Spirit. You will never call on the Holy Spirit in vain. Indeed, in the matter of spiritual direction, the role of the confessor is, above all, to prepare the soul for the action of the Holy Spirit.

There is no question of denying the importance of human effort, or of minimizing the part played by generosity, constancy, and pru-

Christ the ideal of the Priest, chapter XVI, section 2.
[1] Romans 8:26.

dence in our spiritual lives. I am fully persuaded of the value of these elements, but they must not make us lose sight of the supernatural side.

This point is of such capital importance that I would like to insist on it. There is a striking text in the epistle, of St. Paul: "No one can say 'Jesus is Lord,' except in the Holy Spirit." Do these words mean that we are incapable of pronouncing with out lips the words "Jesus is Lord," or that we cannot understand their literal sense? Certainly not. We are able to do this. But in order to pronounce this sacred name and to attain to the Person of Jesus in a salutary manner with Christian hope and charity, we must be moved from on high. The Council of Orange has defined that without the illumination and inspiration of the Holy Spirit, we can do nothing which is efficacious for our salvation. This, indeed, is our faith.

According to St. Thomas, we must acknowledge that God alone communicates to man the gifts of His grace. As it is only fire which can spread fire, so it is only God who can make creatures participate in His own nature, unite them to Himself. He deifies them. This birth of grace in us proceeds from the entire Holy Trinity, but, as an operation of love, it is appropriated to the Person of the Holy Spirit. This same communication of the divine life can, however, quite properly be envisaged as the work of Christ, whose sacred humanity is the efficient cause—not the principal but the instrumental efficient cause—of all grace bestowed on men.[2]

When Our Lord was living on earth, all could certainly approach Him. Had He not come down to us for the salvation of all? And yet, what a difference of attitude was there among those who did approach Him! Some, like the Pharisees, had their hearts hardened and closed to Him. Others perceived something of the mystery of His Person and of His mission. They believed in Him and attached themselves to Him.

What is the explanation of this difference? There are many incidents in the Scriptures which make it clear, commencing with the very start of Jesus' life on earth. Mary visits her cousin Elizabeth and the latter exclaims, "Blessed art thou among women and blessed is the fruit of thy womb!" Who gave Elizabeth this penetrating

[2] St. Thomas, *Summa* 1a 2ae q. 112, art. 1; 3 a q. 64, a.1. Cf. the extensive and penetrating treatment of this subject in chapter 4 of Marmion: *Christ the Life of the Soul*, "Christ the efficient Cause of all Grace."

insight? The Holy Spirit had filled her soul.[3] At the time of the Presentation of Jesus in the temple in Jerusalem, the old man Simeon recognizes the Messiah in the Child of the Virgin. Under what inspiration is he acting? He had come into the temple moved by the Holy Spirit.[4]

There can be little doubt that the sick, who went with such confidence to the Lord to be cured, were also under the influence of this hidden but efficacious impulse of this same Holy Spirit. It was He who led the Magdalen to repentance when she bathed the feet of Christ with tears. He inspired St. Peter and the other disciples to leave their nets to follow Jesus. It was He who invited St. John to lay his head on the bosom of Jesus and to accompany Him to the foot of the Cross.

We must realize that there exists for us a contact, a union, with Jesus which is as intimate, as immediate, as fruitful, as the one of which we have been speaking. It is the contact of faith. It is the Holy Spirit alone who can cause this salutary contact in us. How does He do it? He does it when by efficacious grace He makes the soul capable of believing, hoping, and loving, supernaturally.

As long as Christ lived on this earth His divinity remained hidden, but his humanity was visible. It exercised of itself a certain attraction; it was not an object of faith. At present we cannot reach Jesus in His human nature, or in His divine nature, except by faith alone. This is the divine plan. All our relations with Christ must be founded on this adherence of faith.

This contact of faith is a necessary condition if the divine gifts are to descend upon us. " He who believes in me," Jesus declares, " from within him there shall flow rivers of living waters." And it is noteworthy that the Evangelist adds that the Saviour " said this of the Spirit whom they who believed in him were to receive."[5] That vivifying contact with Jesus in faith is only effected by the gift of the Holy Spirit. It is possible to approach very close to the tabernacle of the altar, and yet remain very far away from Christ. On the other hand, if the influence of the Holy Spirit embraces our lives, contact is established, union effected, and we are near to Jesus, indeed.

The Holy Spirit is the bond between the Father and the Son. He is also the bond between Christ and us. We can then understand,

[3] Luke 1:41.   [4] Luke 2:27.   [5] John 7:39.

therefore, how important it is that we should at all times be subject
to His sanctifying action in our spiritual lives.

24. Beginning the Spiritual Life

T H E soul is not always in the same state. It is necessary to take this
into account in order to fix the habitual subject of our intercourse
with God.

As you know, ascetic tradition distinguishes three stages or states
of perfection:—the purgative way, or that of beginners; the illuminative way, where the fervent advance; and the unitive way,
belonging to perfect souls. These states are thus named according as
such or such a characteristic predominates, although not exclusively.
First there is the labour of purifying the soul, then of its illumination, and finally its state of union with God. It goes without saying
that the habitual nature of prayer varies according to the stage the
soul is in.

Therefore, reservation made of the attraction of the Holy Spirit,
and of the aptitudes of the soul, a beginner in spiritual ways ought to
try to acquire the habit of mental prayer by personal effort.[1]
Although the Holy Spirit helps us powerfully in our relations with
our heavenly Father, His action is not produced in the soul independently of certain conditions resulting from our nature.

The Holy Spirit leads us according to our nature. We are intelligence and will, but we only will the good we know; affection is only
felt towards the good shown by the intelligence. In order to attach
ourselves fully to God—and is not that the best fruit of prayer?—
we must know God as perfectly as possible. That is why, says St.
Thomas, " all that renders faith true is ordered towards charity."[2]

At the beginning, then, of its seeking after God, the soul ought to
store up intellectual principles and knowledge of our faith. Why?
Because without that, one will not know what to say and the prayer

---

Christ the life of the soul, part 2, chapter X, section 3.

[1] Note that the term " mental prayer " is used by design, not the term " meditation ". Meditation is an act of the intellect and is actually only the forward to
prayer, helpful in a greater or lesser degree, depending on the state of soul and
the action of the Holy Spirit.

[2] St. Thomas, *Commentary on 1 Timothy*, chapter I, lect. 2.

will degenerate into vague reverie, without fruit or depth, or else will become an exercise full of weariness that the soul will soon abandon.

This knowledge has first of all to be stored up; then, afterwards, maintained, renewed, and increased. How is this to be done? By applying oneself for some time, with the aid of a book, to prolonged reflection on some point of Revelation. The soul consecrates a period, longer or shorter according to its aptitudes, to considering in detail the chief articles of faith. The result is that, in these successive reflections, the necessary notions are gained that serve as a point of departure for prayer. This is like preparing and providing the raw material from which the Holy Spirit can build within our souls.

This purely discursive work must not be confounded with prayer. It is only the introduction, useful and necessary to enlighten, guide, render pliant or sustain the intelligence, but an introduction all the same. Prayer only begins at the moment when the will, set on fire with love, enters supernaturally into contact with the Divine Good, yielding itself lovingly to God in order to please Him and fulfill His precepts and desire.

It is in the heart that prayer essentially dwells. It is said of the Blessed Virgin that she kept the words of Jesus "in her heart."[3] When Our Lord taught His apostles to pray, He did not bid them apply themselves to such or such reasoning, but to tell the love of their hearts as children—when you pray, say "Father." St. Augustine says that the petitions Christ has instructed us to make are the model of what the desires of our hearts should be.[4] A soul—we are here only making a supposition—that would regularly confine itself to the work of intellectual reasoning, even on matters of faith, would not be applying itself to prayer.

This is what the Abbé Saudreau, whose ascetical works are well known, has written on this subject. "Let us note well that petition is the chief part of prayer, or rather, prayer only begins with this. As long as the soul does not turn towards God to speak to Him" to praise Him, to bless and glorify Him, to delight in His perfections, to make supplication and yield itself to His guidance, "it may, it is true, meditate, but it is not applying itself to mental prayer. We see people sometimes mistaken in this and, in an exercise of half an hour, pass all their time in reflecting, without saying anything to

[3] Luke 2:51.   [4] St. Augustine, *Sermons*, 56, c.3.

God. Even when they have added holy desires and generous resolutions, still, that is not praying. Doubtless the mind has not been acting alone, the heart is enkindled with ardour and borne along to what is good, but it does not pour itself out into the Heart of God. Such meditations are almost fruitless; they very quickly bring fatigue and very often, also, discouragement and the relinquishment of this holy exercise."[5]

Simple reading, interspersed with the deliberate intercourse with God, can be a mighty aid for beginners, but the exclusive intellectual exercise, where reason alone enters, must be avoided during the time set aside for mental prayer. The former includes study and prayer; the latter is only a lesson, a study period. But, in order to guard against illusions (and sloth) the soul ought necessarily to be aided by the counsels of an enlightened director.

25. Progress in Prayer

IT is a fact proved by experience that the more a soul advances in spiritual ways, the more the discursive work of reasoning is reduced. Why is this? Because the soul is now filled with the knowledge of Christian truths. It is no longer needful to store up notions of faith. These have already been gained. There is nothing more to do but maintain and renew them by the reading of holy books.

It follows that long considerations are far less necessary to one all permeated with Divine truths. Such a soul possesses all the material elements of prayer and can now enter into contact with God without discursive labour. This law of experience naturally allows of exceptions that must be carefully respected. There are some far advanced in spiritual ways who can never enter into prayer without the help of a book; reading serves to put them in the right atmosphere for prayer; it would be a mistake for them to do without it.

There are others who can only commune with God through vocal prayer; they would be ill at ease if led into another way. However, as

---

[5] Saudeau, *The Degrees of the spiritual life.* Cf, also, among recent writers, Fenton: *Theology of Prayer,* and McSorley: *Primer of Prayer.*
Christ the Life of the Soul, part 2, chapter X, sections 4 and 5.

a general rule, it remains true that in the same measure that one progresses in the light of faith and in fidelity, the action of the Holy Spirit increases within the soul, and there is ever less need of having recourse to reasoning in order to find God.

This is above all true, as experience shows, of those whose knowledge of Christ's mysteries is deeper and more extensive. Listen to what St. Paul wrote to the early Christians. "Let the word of Christ dwell in you abundantly."[1] The great apostle desires this in order that the faithful may teach one another "in all wisdom." But this exhortation is of value, too, for our own intercourse with God. Why so?

The word of Christ is contained in the Gospels which, with the letters of St. Paul and St. John, are the most supernatural (because inspired) exposition of Christ's mysteries. The child of God finds therein the best title to his Divine adoption and the Model he has to imitate. Christ Jesus shows Himself to us in His earthly existence, in His doctrine, in His love. We there find the best source of the knowledge of God, of His nature, His perfections, and His works. "For God, who commanded light to shine out of darkness, has shone in our hearts, to give enlightenment concerning the knowledge of the glory of God, shining on the face of Christ Jesus."[2]

Christ is God's great Revelation to the world. God tells us, "This is my beloved Son, hear Him!" It is as if He said to us, "If you wish to please me, look at My Son; look at My Son, imitate Him; I ask nothing besides this, for in this is your predestination that you be conformed to My Son."

Look at Our Lord and contemplate His actions; that is the most direct way of knowing God. To see Him is to see the Father; He is only one with His Father; He only does what is pleasing to His Father. Each of His actions is the object of His Father's complacency and we should delight in making it the object of our contemplation.

"Were you at the summit of contemplation," writes St. Teresa, "take no other road than that of regarding the holy Humanity of Jesus. One walks with assurance along that road. Our Lord is for us the source of every good; He Himself will teach us. Look at His life; He is the best Model." And the saints adds, "If instead of taking the habit of having (in prayer) this holy Humanity ever

[1] Col. 3:16.   [2] 2 Cor. 4:6.

present before us—and would to God it was ever present—we purposely and deliberately do precisely the contrary, once again that is what I disapprove of. To act thus is to walk on air, as they say. And, in fact, however full of God a soul may believe itself to be, it lacks a point of support. Being men, it is very advantageous to us, as long as we are in this life, to consider God made man."[3]

But Christ has not only acted. He has also spoken. " I spoke of all that Jesus did and taught from the beginning until the day on which he was taken up, after he had given commandments through the Holy Spirit."[4] All His words reveal the Divine secrets to us. He only speaks of that which He beholds, and His words, as He himself tells us, are for us, " spirit and life." They contain life for the soul, not in the manner of the sacraments, but they bear with them the light that enlightens and the strength that sustains. The actions and words of Jesus are for us motives of confidence and love, and principles of action.

That is why the words of Christ ought to " abide " in us so as to become in us principles of life; that is the reason, too, why it is useful for the soul that desires to live by prayer to read the Gospels constantly, and to follow the Church, our Mother, when she represents to us the actions and recalls the words of Jesus in the course of the liturgical cycle.

In making all the stages of the life of Christ, her Bridegroom and our Elder Brother, pass before our eyes, the Church supplies us with abundant food for prayer. A soul that thus follows Our Lord step by step possesses, presented by the Church, the material elements necessary for prayer. It is there that the faithful soul finds, above all, the " Word of God," and, being united to Him by faith, it brings forth supernatural fruit. For the least word of Jesus Christ is for the soul a light, and a source of life and grace.

It is the Holy Spirit who makes us understand these words and all they contain for each one. What did Jesus say to His apostles before ascending into heaven? " But the Advocate, the Holy Spirit, whom the Father will send in My name, He will teach you all things, and bring to your mind whatever I have said to you."[5] *That* word is ever being fulfilled, for Christ's words do not pass away. Christ, the Incarnate Word, together with His Father, gave us His Spirit on the

---

[3] St. Teresa, *Life by herself*, chapter 22.   [4] Acts 1:1-2.
[5] John 14:26.

day of our baptism, which made us children of God—children of the heavenly Father and Christ's own brethren.

This Spirit abides with us. " You shall know Him, because He will dwell with you, and be in you."[6] And what does He do in us, this Divine Spirit, the Spirit of Truth? He brings to our mind the words of Jesus. Our Lord Himself tells us so. What does this mean? It means that when we contemplate the actions and mysteries of Christ Jesus, either in reading the Gospel or a " Life " of Our Lord, or when, under the Church's guidance, in the course of the liturgical year, one day it happens that some word, such as we may have read and re-read many times without its having particularly struck us, suddenly stands out in supernatural relief in a way we have not hitherto known.

It is a flash of light that the Holy Spirit makes all at once to rise from the depth of the soul. It is like a sudden revelation of a source of life hitherto unknown or unsuspected, like a new and wider horizon that opens out before the eyes of the soul. It is like a new world that the Spirit discovers to us. He whom the liturgy names " the finger of God " in the hymn *Veni Creator,* engraves this Divine word on the soul, there ever to remain a light and a principle of action. If the soul is humble and attentive, this Divine Word works in it, silent but fruitful.

When we are faithful, every day, to consecrate a time, longer or shorter according to our aptitudes and duties of state, in speaking with the heavenly Father, in gathering up His inspirations and listening to what the Holy Spirit " brings to mind," then the words of Christ, the words of the Word, as St. Augustine calls them, go on multiplying, inundating the soul with divine Light and opening out in it fountains of life so that the soul's thirst may be ever assuaged. In this is realized the promise of Christ Jesus, that if any man should thirst, and come to him and drink, there should spring up within him that believes, " rivers of living water." And St. John adds, " He said this, however, of the Spirit whom they who believed in him were to receive."[7]

The soul, in return, constantly expresses itself in acts of faith, repentance, compunction, confidence, love, complacency, and submission to the will of the heavenly Father. It moves in an atmosphere that maintains it more and more in union with God. Prayer becomes

[6] John 14:17.   [7] John 7:37-38.

G

its breath, its life; it is filled with the spirit of prayer. Prayer then becomes a state, and the soul can find its God at will, even in the midst of many occupations.

The moments in the day that the soul consecrates exclusively to the formal exercise of prayer are only the intensifying of this state in which it remains habitually, but gently, united to God, speaking to Him interiorly and listening to the voice from on high.

This state is more than the simple presence of God. It is an intimate intercourse, full of love, in which the soul speaks to God, sometimes with the lips, most often from the heart, and remains intimately united to Him, despite the variety of the day's work and occupations. There are many souls, simple and upright, who, faithful to the attraction of the Holy Spirit, reach this desirable state.

Then, if it pleases the Supreme Goodness, God leads the soul beyond the common frontiers of the supernatural so as to give Himself to it in mysterious communications where the natural faculties, raised by the Divine action, receive, under the influence of the gifts of the Holy Spirit, notably the gifts of understanding and wisdom, a higher mode of operation. Mystic writers describe the different degrees of these Divine operations which are sometimes accompanied by extraordinary phenomena, such as ecstasy.

We can in nowise reach such degrees of prayer and union with God by our own efforts. They depend solely on the free and supreme will of God.

May we, however, desire them? Not if it concerns the accidental phenomena that may accompany contemplation, such as ecstasy, revelations, stigmata, etc. That would be presumption and temerity.

But, if it concerns what is the very substance itself of contemplation, that is to say, the most pure, simple and perfect knowledge which God gives therein of Himself and His perfections, and the intense love the soul derives from this knowledge, then, I would say to you, desire with all your strength to possess a high degree of prayer and to enjoy perfect contemplation. For God is the principal author of our sanctity. He acts powerfully in these communications, and not to desire them would be not to desire to love God with our whole heart, our whole soul, our whole mind, and our whole strength.[8]

And, then, what is it that gives to our life all its value, that deter-

[8] Mark 12:30.

mines for our part—reservation being made of Divine action—the degrees of holiness to which we are to attain? It is, as I have constantly said, the purity and intensity of the love with which we pass through this life and perform our actions. Now, beyond the direct action of the sacraments, this purity and intensity of charity come to us abundantly in prayer, and that is why it is so useful for us. That, too, is why we may legitimately desire to attain a high degree of prayer.

It is clear, however, that we ought to subject this desire to the will of God. He alone knows what is best for our souls. While sparing neither our efforts to remain generously and humbly faithful to present grace, nor our ardent aspirations towards higher perfection, it is extremely important to keep always in peace, assured as we are of God's goodness and wisdom in regard to each of us.

" Lord, teach us to pray! "

26. Growth in the Spirit

You may perhaps say: Have we not already received the Holy Spirit at Baptism, and yet more specially in the Sacrament of Confirmation?

Assuredly we have, but we can always receive Him more abundantly. We can always receive from Him clearer light, greater strength. He can always make deeper well-springs of consolation rise up in our souls, and enkindle within our hearts a more intense love.

And this fruitful working of the Holy Spirit within us can be renewed not only during the holy days of Pentecost, but moreover, each time that we receive a sacrament we receive an increase of grace and the entire Holy Trinity comes and dwells in the soul.[1] The Holy Spirit comes to dwell within us; He remains to sanctify us, to guide all our supernatural activity. He enriches us, bestows upon us His gifts of wisdom and of understanding of holy counsel and of fortitude, of knowledge, of piety and of fear of the Lord which make us act as children of God. " For whoever are led by the Spirit of God, they are the sons of God."[2]

Christ in His mysteries, chapter XVII, section 5.   [1] John 14:23.
[2] Romans 8:14.

He dwells in us, a divine Guest full of love and kindness. He makes His abode in our hearts that He may help and strengthen us. He will leave us only if we have the misfortune to drive Him from our souls by mortal sin. To drive out this Spirit of love, by preferring the creature to Him in an absolute manner, is what St. Paul calls "extinguishing the Spirit."[3] Moreover, let us follow the Apostle's counsel and not " grieve "[4] the Spirit. Let us not resist His inspirations by any fully deliberate fault, however slight, by willfully replying " no " to the good He suggests to us.

His action is extremely delicate, and when the soul resists Him deliberately and frequently, the soul forces Him little by little to be silent. Then comes the standstill in the path that leads to holiness! Great risk is incurred even of leaving the way of salvation. What can such a soul do without light to enlighten, without a master to guide, without strength to sustain or joy to transport it?

Let us be faithful to this Spirit Who comes, with the Father and the Son, to take up His abode in us. " Do you not know," says St. Paul, " that you are the temple of God and that the Spirit of God dwells in you? "[5] Each increase of grace is like a new reception of this Divine Guest, a new taking possession of our souls by Him, a new embrace of love.

And how beneficial are these workings in the faithful soul! He makes us " know the Father "[6] and, by making Him known, He produces in the soul the gift of piety, the attitude of adoration and love which it ought ever to preserve towards the heavenly Father.

Listen to what St. Paul so explicitly says. " But in like manner the Spirit also helps our weakness. For we do not know what we should pray for as we ought, but the Spirit himself pleads for us with unutterable groanings."[7] And what is this prayer? " You have received a spirit of adoption as sons, by virtue of which we cry ' Abba! Father! ' The Spirit Himself gives testimony to our spirit, that we are sons of God."[8]

He makes us also " know the Son."[9] He manifests Jesus to us. He is this inward Master who makes us penetrate into the meaning of His words and mysteries. " He will glorify me," says Jesus, " because he will receive of what is mine and declare it to you."[10]

[3] 1 Thess. 5:19.   [4] Ephesians 4:30.   [5] 1 Cor. 3:16.
[6] Hymn *Veni Creator*.   [7] Romans 8:26.   [8] Romans 8:15-16.
[9] Hymn *Veni Creator*.   [10] St. John 16:14.

By making divine knowledge abound in us, by keeping us in the presence of Jesus, by inspiring us ever to do what is pleasing to Him, He causes Christ to reign in us. By His infinitely delicate and sovereignly efficacious action, He forms Jesus in us. Is not that the substance of all holiness?

Let us, then, ask Him to enter into us and increase in us the abundance of His gifts. Fervent prayer is the condition of His indwelling in our souls.

Humility is another condition. Let us come before Him with the intimate conviction of our inward poverty. This disposition of soul is excellent in order to receive Him of whom the Church sings "Without Thy help there is nothing in man that is not harmful to him."[11] Let us borrow, moreover, from the Church, these fervent aspirations: "Come, Spirit of love; come, Thou solace in sorrow, wash away our stains, water our dryness, heal our wounds. Bend that which is stubborn in us, melt that which is frozen, and rule our wandering steps."[12]

Despite our miseries, let us invoke the Holy Spirit. On account of these very miseries, He will hear us.

And since He is one with the Father and the Son, let us say likewise to the Father: Father send to us, in the name of Thy Son Jesus, the Spirit of love that He may fill us with the intimate sense of our divine filiation. And Thou, O Jesus, our High Priest, now sitting at Thy Father's right hand, intercede for us, so that this mission of the Spirit, whom thou didst promise to us and didst merit for us, may be abundant; that it may be an impetuous river making glad the city of souls; or rather, according to Thine own words "a fountain of water, springing up unto life everlasting."

27. The life of prayer

January 8, 1908. In every soul, three spirits strive for the mastery. The spirit of falsehood and blasphemy who from the beginning ever

[11] Sequence *Veni Sancte Spiritus.*
[12] Sequence *Veni Sancte Spiritus;* Cf, also, Gihr, *An Explanation of the Veni Sancte Spiritus.*

Union with God : various letters of spiritual direction.

suggests the exact contrary of what God whispers. "If you eat of this fruit you shall certainly die," said God. "You shall never die,"[1] was Satan's reply, and in all his suggestions there is only the echo of this first lie.

Then there is the spirit of this world, inclining us to judge things according to the maxims of sense and carnal prudence. The prudence of this world is folly before God.

Then there is the Spirit of God ever whispering in our ears to raise our hearts above nature: "Lift up your hearts!" and to live by faith. "But my just one lives by faith."[2] This Spirit always inclines us towards simple loving faith and abandonment of self into God's hands. It fills us with "peace and joy in believing" and produces the fruits of which St. Paul speaks.

Now, in certain persons the action of these several spirits is more tangible and striking than in others. You will always know them by their fruits, even though Satan may try to clothe himself as an angel of light. Our Lord says that: "By their fruits you will know them."[3] You will recognize these spirits by the fruits they produce in your soul.

God's Spirit, even when He reproaches us or inclines us to confusion or compunction for our sins, ever fills the soul with peace and filial confidence in our heavenly Father. The other spirits dry up the soul, fill us with naturalistic tendencies, or, if it be the spirit of hell, casts gloom and discouragement into our soul. Now just as Eve should have refused to believe or even to listen to the infernal spirit when he contradicted God's testimony, just as she ought to have put him to flight by saying like St. Michael, "Who is like God? Do you think I will pay attention to your hissing lies when they contradict God's word?" So should we.

I recommend to you a great fidelity to the movements of the Holy Spirit. Your baptism and your confirmation have established Him as a living fountain in your soul. Hear His whisperings, and put the other inspirations to flight at once. If you are faithful in this, little by little this Divine Spirit will become your guide and bear you with Him into God's bosom. The Holy Spirit holds the place for us that Jesus did for His apostles during His mortal life. Just as they could have recourse to Him, speak to Him, pray, etc., so He has sent us

[1] Genesis 2:17; 3:4.   [2] Hebrews 10:38.   [3] Matthew 7:16.

another Paraclete to stay with us and teach us all things which He
has told us.[4]

* * *

July 18th, 1917. I am rejoiced to see that the Holy Spirit is
making you understand that we have all in Jesus Christ. For this
knowledge is the grain of mustard seed Our Lord speaks of, which
to begin with is very small, then, on being cultivated, becomes a
great tree.

Here, simply, is what I try to teach:

Jesus Christ is infinite holiness. But, He is not only holy in Himself; He has been given to us to be our holiness. "From Him you
are in Christ Jesus, who has become for us God-given wisdom, and
justice, and sanctification, and redemption."[5]

He is our holiness:

1.   As perfect model: "Predestined to be conformed to the
      image of His Son."[6] God finds in Him all His delights:
      "This is My beloved Son in whom I am well-pleased." He
      finds them in us according to the degree of our likeness to
      Jesus.

2.   As means of union with God. In Jesus the divine nature and
      the human nature are united in oneness of Person, and we
      are united with the Divinity in the measure of our union
      with the Sacred Humanity of Jesus. He is the cornerstone
      making both one.[7] It is by sanctifying grace that this union
      with God is brought about, and this grace is the work of the
      the Blessed Trinity in us.

3.   However the effusion of this grace depends on Jesus Christ:
      a) It is He who merited it;
      b) It is He who applies it through His Sacred Humanity;
      c) This grace tends to reproduce in us the features of
         Jesus Christ;
      d) The more we lean upon Him, the more abundant is
         this grace.

In fact, this grace, poured forth without measure in the

---

[4] John 14:26.   [5] 1 Cor. 1:30.   [6] Romans 8:29.
[7] Cf. Ephesians 2:14, and the antiphon for Dec. 22nd, *O Rex Gentium.*

Sacred Humanity, is communicated to His members in the measure of their union with Him by faith and love. "I am the Vine, you are the branches."[8]

All the graces that we receive tend to make of us, by the grace of adoption what Jesus is by nature—children of God. That is why the *same* Holy Spirit who was, in Jesus, the principle of His whole human life, is given to us: "And because you are sons, God has sent the spirit of His son into our hearts, crying, 'Abba, Father.'"[9] It is this Holy Spirit who achieves in us the image of Jesus and fills us with His life. "The Spirit gives life."[10]

There, in a few words, is all that I know.

*   *   *

October 2nd, 1919. The Holy Spirit is inviting you to passive prayer and you must not extinguish the Spirit by misplaced activity. Nothing is more glorious to God nor more advantageous for us than to give God a free hand in our souls once He indicates His desire to have it. Blosius says that a soul which abandons itself to God's action without reserve, allowing Him to operate as He wishes, does more for His glory and for souls in an hour than others do in years.

Once you feel the attraction to remain in the silence of adoration in God's presence, you must give yourself entirely to the Holy Spirit and remain there in pure faith. If God gives you no feeling, no sentiment, no distinct thought, just be there before Him in silent love. During such moments He operates insensibly in the soul and does more for her perfection than she could in a lifetime by her own thoughts, etc.

If at any moment you feel attracted to petition or other acts, follow this attraction. It is not necessary to pronounce words, or to form distinct thoughts. Just present yourself and your petition in silent prayer before God's face. He sees all that your heart is saying: God hears the desires of the poor.

When you feel invited to remain in silence at Our Lord's feet, like Magdalen, just looking at Him with your heart, without saying anything, don't cast about for any thoughts or reasonings, but just

[8] John 15:5; cf. Council of Trent, 6th session, c.7.
[9] Galatians 4:6.
[10] 2 Cor. 3:6.

remain in loving adoration. Follow the whisperings of the Holy Spirit. If He invites you to beg, beg; if to be silent, remain silent; if to show your misery to God, just do so. Let Him play on the fibres of your heart like a harpist, and draw forth the melody He wishes for the Divine Spouse.[11]

The distractions are only on the surface of your soul. They are a cross, but you must learn to despise them. Your prayer goes on in the hidden depths of your soul, which is, as it were, lying in God's bosom, His essence, and drinking in vast draughts of love and light.

If God ever speaks interior words, be sure to submit them to your director before acting on them.

* * *

October 5th, 1906. I am perfectly certain that despite your unworthiness and littleness, that God means and wishes to unite you very closely to Him. He is Master of His gifts which he bestows freely on whom He wishes. I wish you to give yourself up without fear to the leading of the Holy Spirit. If He unites you even more closely with God, don't resist and don't be afraid. Your misery and unworthiness which God has had the goodness to reveal to you, will protect you against illusions, and will but become more and more manifest to the eyes of your soul.

28. Devotion to the Holy Spirit

WE have considered the action of the Holy Spirit in the Church and in our souls. Like the Divine principle whence it emanates, this action is holy and tends to make us holy. What, then, shall be our devotion towards this Spirit who dwells in us from our baptism and whose virtue within us is, of its nature, so deep and efficacious?

First of all we must often invoke Him. Like the Father and the Son, the Holy Spirit is God; He too desires our holiness. Moreover, it enters into the Divine plan that we should pray to the Holy Spirit as we pray to the Father and the Son to whom He is equal in power

[11] Excerpt from letter of May 29th, 1915.
Christ the Life of the Soul, chapter VI, section 6.

and goodness. The Church is our guide in this. She closes the cycle of solemnities celebrating Christ's mysteries with Pentecost, the feast of the mission of the Holy Spirit. During this time she has wonderful prayers wherewith to ask grace from the Divine Spirit, aspirations full of love, such as the *Veni Sancte Spiritus*.

O Infinite Love, proceeding from the Father and the Son, give me the spirit of adoption; teach me always to acts as a true child of God. Abide in me; grant that I may abide in Thee so that I may love Thee as Thou hast loved first. I am nothing without Thee. " Without Thy Divine action there is nothing of good in man! "[1] Of myself, I am good for nothing, but keep me united to Thee, fill me with Thy love that I may remain so united through Thee to the Father and the Son!

Let us often ask for a greater share in the Holy Spirit's gifts, " the sacred seven-fold gifts." We ought to thank Him too, and return humble thanks.

If Christ Jesus has merited for us, and merited all that we receive, it is by His Spirit that he guides and directs us. When we say that Christ guides us by the Holy Spirit, we do not say that the Holy Spirit is an instrument. He is God, the cause of grace. We mean by this that the Holy Spirit is the principle (for us) of grace, Himself, proceeding from a principle, from the Father and the Son. Jesus Christ, as Word, sends us the Holy Spirit.[2]

It is through the magnificent liberality of His Spirit that we hold those abundant graces which make us, little by little, like to Jesus. How can we fail to testify often of our gratitude to this Guest whose loving and efficacious presence fills us with such precious benefits? The first homage we must offer to this Spirit, who with the Father and the Son is God, is to believe with a practical faith in His Divinity, His power and His goodness.

Next, let us take care not to oppose His action within us. " Do not extinguish the Spirit," says St. Paul.[3] And again, " Do not grieve the Holy Spirit of God."[4] As I have said, the action of the Spirit in the soul is delicate because it is an action of completeness, of perfection. His touches are of infinite delicacy. We must be watchful not to oppose the workings of this Divine Spirit by our

[1] From the hymn *Veni Sancte Spiritus*.
[2] St. Thomas, *Summa* 1a, q.45, a 6, at 2nd.
[3] 1 Thes. 5:19.   [4] Ephes. 4:30.

levity, our voluntary dissipation, our carelessness, or wilful deliberate resistance, by an ill-regulated attachment to our own judgement. "Be not wise in your own conceits."[5]

If the things of God, do not trust to human wisdom, for then the Holy Spirit will relinquish you to this natural prudence which, as you know, St. Paul says is "foolishness" in God's sight.[6] This action of the Holy Spirit is quite compatible with those imperfections which so often overtake us by surprise and which we regret, compatible, too, with our infirmities, human limitations and temptations. Our native poverty does not repel the Holy Spirit; He is the "Father of the poor" as the Church calls Him in the *Veni Sancte Spiritus*.

That which is incompatible with His action is calculated resistance to His inspirations. Why is this? First because the Spirit proceeds from love, He is Love itself. And yet, although His love for us is incommensurable, and His action infinitely powerful, the Holy Spirit absolutely respects our liberty and does not compel our free will. We have the sad privilege of being able to resist Him; but nothing thwarts love like obstinate resistance to its advances.

Then, it is above all by His gifts that the Holy Spirit guides us in the path of holiness and makes us live as children of God. In His gifts, it is the Holy Spirit who urges and determines the soul to act.[7] The soul's part is certainly not to remain entirely passive, but to be ready to receive Divine inspiration, to listen to it, and to be faithful to it.

Nothing blunts the action of the Holy Spirit in us like a rigid, unbending attitude in regard to those inward movements which bear us Godwards, and urge us to the observance of His commandments, to the accomplishment of His good pleasure, to charity, humility, and confidence. To reply "no" voluntarily, deliberately, even in little things, impedes the Holy Spirit's action within us. It becomes less strong and more rare, and the soul remains at an ordinary degree, a mediocre level of holiness; its supernatural life lacks intensity. "Do not grieve the Holy Spirit of God."[8]

And if these infidelities are multiplied, and become frequent and habitual, the Holy Spirit is silent. The soul thus given over to itself,

---

[5] Romans 12:15.   [6] 1 Cor. 3:19.
[7] St. Thomas, *Summa*, 2ae 2a, q. 52, a 2, at 1.   [8] Ephes. 4:30.

without guide and inward support in the path of salvation and perfection, is very near to becoming the prey of the prince of darkness;
it is the death of charity. " Do not extinguish the Spirit,"[9] for He is
like a fire of love burning within our souls.[10]

Rather, let us remain, in the measure of our weakness, but with
generosity, faithful to the Spirit of Truth who is also the Spirit of
Holiness. Let us be souls promptly docile to the touches of this
Spirit. What deep joy and what inward liberty a soul tastes that thus
gives itself up to the action of the Holy Spirit!

This Divine Spirit will cause us to bear fruits of holiness pleasing
to God. As the Divine Artist—the "finger of God's right hand"[11]
—He will, with infinitely delicate touches, complete in us the work
of Jesus, or rather, He will form Jesus within us, as He formed the
Holy Humanity of Jesus, so that by His workings, we may reproduce in ourselves, to the glory of the Father, the traits of that Divine
sonship that we have in Christ Jesus.[12]

29. Invoking the Holy Spirit

Y o u know that indelible marks are graven on the soul by the sacraments of baptism, confirmation, and holy orders. These characters are
permanent in the soul. They are permanent testimonies of our
dependence on Christ which can, at all times, whenever we will, be
presented before God. Thanks to them, we can recall within us the
Holy Spirit and thus revive the supernatural effects proper to each of
these sacraments. St. Paul teaches this formally for holy orders: " I
admonish thee," he writes to Timothy, " to stir up the grace of God
which is in thee by the laying on of my hands."[1]

At baptism, said Jesus, man is born again to a new life by virtue
of water and the Holy Spirit.[2] From that time, the Spirit of Christ
dwells in the baptized soul and preserves it. " And because you are
sons, God has sent the Spirit of His Son into our hearts."[3]

---

[9] I Thes. 5 :19.   [10] Hymn, *Veni Creator*.   [11] Hymn *Veni Creator*.
[12] St. Thomas, *Summa*, 3a, q.32, a.1.
   Christ the ideal of the Priest, chapter XVI, section 3. Cf also *Send Forth Thy
Spirit*, a prayer-book compiled and composed by Bishop Charles Francis Buddy, and
published by St. Paul Editions, Boston.
   [1] 2 Timothy 1 :6.   [2] John 3 :5.   [3] Galatians 4 :6.

Of its own accord our baptismal character is already crying out to heaven. It is pleading for us. Let us rely on it in our invocation of the Holy Spirit, asking Him to teach us to pray as children of God, to treat with our Sovereign Lord as with a Father, asking Him to inspire us to live in all things in accordance with the fullness of our baptismal grace, according to the example of Jesus, the only-Son, by nature.

What is it that Christ does at confirmation by the ministry of His bishop? He extends his hand over the heads of those to be confirmed and then anoints them with chrism. Making the sign of the cross on their foreheads, he says, " I sign thee with the sign of the cross." This visible sign of the Cross represents the invisible character imprinted on the soul. The imprint of Christ, glorious in the sight of the angels and saints, is graven on the soul forever.

The bishop continues the ceremony, "I confirm thee with the chrism of salvation . . ." That is to say, I make you strong, I complete the effect of baptism, I make you a perfect Christian, a soldier of Jesus Christ, ready to defend His cause. The holy chrism spread on the forehead represents the unction of the Holy Spirit which enters into souls and extends itself in them to give them strength.

Invoking this character, we must pray to the Holy Spirit that in all the struggles and difficulties of life, He may give us the strength to be faithful soldiers of Christ, proud to serve Him and zealous to defend and to extend His kingdom.

In the sacrament of holy orders, a third sacred mark, that of ordination, is ever present in the depths of the priest's very being, itself a constant invocation of the Holy Spirit. Every day, strong in faith, the priest raises his hands towards heaven, exhibiting to the Lord a soul marked with the seal of Christ.

We must have a vivid appreciation of the characters of these sacraments. Take full advantage of them, for our whole supernatural life consists in the persevering development in ourselves of the graces proper to our vocations, our state in life.

This invocation can find its expression in a simple movement of the heart, in prayer to the Holy Spirit, or in one of those burning aspirations in which the liturgy of Pentecost is so rich. "Come, Father of the poor . . . source of graces . . . sweet guest of souls . . . heal our wounds."

It is an excellent practice, in the course of the day, to renew our fervour by means of these aspirations. The Sign of the Cross, and the doxology " Glory be to the Father, and to the Son, and to the Holy Spirit . . ." are dynamos, properly used, to renew our fervour. The Blessed Peter Fabre of the Society of Jesus carried this practice so far that even during the divine Office, between the psalms, he used to address himself mentally to the Father, saying: " Heavenly Father, give me your Spirit." Father Willy Doyle, a holy Jesuit chaplain killed in World War I, carried the practice of frequent aspirations to a high point.

We must keep our souls under the influence of the Holy Spirit. In a symphony, every member of the orchestra is careful to follow with perfect docility the direction of the conductor who now quickens, now moderates the movement. If the spirit of God found a like sub- missiveness in us, He would touch the most profound chords of our hearts and draw from the the praise which God expects of us.

This is so true, that, in the words of St. John Chrysostom, every time that the Christian people apply themselves to the recitation of the psalms, they become like a lyre ready to vibrate under the hand of the Spirit, their divine moderator.[4] The psalter is like a divine harp which the Church gives us that we may sing the praises of Him whom we love.

We find in it the perfect expression of those sentiments of faith, hope, and love which we should entertain in regard to Our Father in heaven. Only God knows Himself perfectly; only God knows how He should be praised. In the psalms, inspired by the Holy Spirit, He Himself dictates to us the words in which He is pleased to be praised by us.

Whenever we invoke the Holy Spirit, we call forth from the Father a fresh outpouring of Pentecostal love.

[4] St. John Chrysostom: *De Lazaro.*

30. The Holy Spirit and Marmion

March 3rd, 1900. When the Word espoused His humanity He brought it a dowry. As the Spouse was God, the dowry was necessarily divine.

According to the Fathers and Doctors of the Church, the dowry which the Word presented to His humanity was the Holy Spirit, who proceeds from Him as from the Father and who is the substantial plenitude of sanctity . . . For some time I have felt a special and ever increasing attraction to the Holy Spirit. I have a great desire to be guided, led, moved in all things by the Spirit of Jesus.

Our Lord, as man, did nothing except under the impulse of the Holy Spirit and in dependence on Him. Thus it is that while, in virtue of the hypostatic union, it was the Word, and the Word alone, who possessed the sacred humanity, He never acted in it or made it accomplish anything except through the Holy Spirit.

We have received the same Spirit in baptism and confirmation and since we are sons, God has sent the spirit of His Son into our hearts. St. Paul speaks constantly of the Spirit of Jesus which guided and enlightened him in all things.

Everything in our activity which comes from this Holy Spirit is holy: for what is born of the Spirit is of the Spirit. It is the Spirit which gives life. The man who delivers himself up without reserve or resistance to this Spirit, the Father of the poor and the Giver of gifts, will be infallibly led by the same road as Jesus, and in the manner which Jesus wills for each individual. This Spirit impelled Elizabeth to praise Mary, and Mary is impelled by the same Spirit of Jesus to proclaim the glory of God.

The Holy Spirit impels us to approach the Father as Jesus approaches Him. By the Spirit of adoption we, too, can call out "Father!" The Holy Spirit moves us to glorify Jesus and give testimony of Him; to pray as one should, forming requests in our hearts with His unutterable groanings. He impels us to humility and to compunction, because He is the remission of all sins. It is through

Christ the ideal of the Priest. Appendix: Dom Marmion's life as a Priest, section 16. These are notes from Abbot Marmion's personal writings and all except the last one used here were written while he was at the Louvain.

Him that we do good to souls: the apostles accomplished so little before Pentecost. It is He who renders all our activity fruitful.

I shall try to live in this Holy Spirit.

October 5th, 1906. God seeks those who seek Him in spirit and in truth. The Holy Spirit is the Spirit of the Father and the Son, and those who allow themselves to be guided by Him are seeking the Father and the Son in truth. He is the Holy Spirit because all His inspirations are infinitely holy; He is the same Spirit who inspired Jesus in all His actions and in all His thoughts. It is by union with Him that the interior life of Jesus is formed in our hearts. He is the Father of the poor, and He unites Himself constantly to those who live in adoration and in the spirit of self-abasement in His presence. He is the Spirit of holy charity, and, being the same in all men, He unites us in holy love.

Pentecost, 1907. It is by the Holy Spirit that Jesus united Himself to His Father. This same Spirit dwells in our hearts: " He dwells among you and He will be in you." He is entirely dedicated to the Father and the Son, and He carries with Himself into the bosom of the Father and the Son all creation, which He loves in His " procession."

The more we abandon ourselves to this Holy Spirit of love, the more are all the tendencies of our being directed towards God. There are three spirits which are liable to take possession of us: the spirit of darkness, the human spirit, and the Holy Spirit. It is very important to distinguish the action of these spirits so that we may deliver ourselves up only to the Spirit of God.

November 15th, 1908. It seems to me that the more intimately I am united to our divine Lord, the more He attracts me to His Father —the more also He seeks to fill me with His own filial spirit. This is the whole spirit of the new law: that we have not received a spirit of fearful servitude, but we have been given the Spirit of adoption as sons whereby we can say Abba! Father!

Letter of April 9th, 1917. During this Paschal season, the Church invites us to receive and revive in ourselves the grace of our baptism, as St. Paul exhorts Timothy to revive the grace of his ordination to the priesthood. The three sacraments: baptism, confirmation and holy orders, leave us the mark of the Spirit, the pledge of the Spirit, a pledge which always calls down on us the grace of the sacrament.

Baptism contains all sanctity in embryo. 1. Grace: participation in the divine nature, residing in the essence of the soul. 2. Theological virtues: faith, hope and charity in the powers of the soul. 3. Gifts of the Holy Spirit. 4. infused moral virtues. All these gifts are the equipment of the Child of the heavenly Father, redeemed by Jesus Christ.

Confirmation strengthens and perfects this seed of life. The Holy Eucharist provides its nourishment; faith is its root and its life: the just man lives by faith.

All the rites and prayers employed in the administration of these sacraments have lasting effects which we can revive by faith and in the Holy Spirit. I frequently make my mental prayer by contemplating the heavenly Father in Jesus Christ in order to beg Him to renew in me all that the Church has asked for me and effected in me on the occasion of the reception of these sacraments. This is my refuge unless the Spirit of Christ attracts me to other activities.

31. Our Lady of the Holy Spirit

G O D is, by His very nature, infinitely generous. It is the essence of goodness to diffuse itself; infinite goodness is urged in an infinite manner to give itself. God is this boundless goodness. Revelation teaches us that there are between the Divine Persons, from the Father to the Son, and from the Father and the Son to the Holy Spirit, infinite communications wherein God finds the full satisfaction of this natural tendency of His Being to give itself.

But beyond this natural communication of infinite Goodness, there is another, arising from God's *free* love towards the creature. The fullness of being and of good that is God has overflowed beyond, through love. And how has this come to pass? God has chosen in the first place to give Himself in an altogether special manner to a creature by uniting it in a personal manner with His Word. This gift of God to a creature is unique. It makes of this creature chosen by the Holy Trinity the very Son of God. "Thou art my Son; this day have I begotten Thee."[1] It is Christ, it is the Word united personally and in an indissoluble manner to a human nature, like to

Christ in His mysteries, chapter IX, passim.
[1] Psalm 2:7.

ours in all things, excepting sin. It is Christ who is born of a woman[2] of the seed of David.[3]

From us He asks this human nature. It is as if the eternal Father were saying to us: Give Me your nature for my Son, and I, in return, will give to this nature, and through it, to every man of good will, a participation in My divinity.

For God thus communicates Himself to Christ only in order to give Himself, through Christ, to us all. God's plan is that Christ should receive the divinity in its fullness and that we should draw, in our turn, from this fullness. "Of His fullness we have all received."[4]

Such is the communication of God's goodness to the world. "For God so loved the world that He gave his only-begotten Son."[5] This is the wonderful order that rules the exchange between God and humanity.

But, who is it, out of all others, that God will ask to be a mother to this humanity to which He wills to unite Himself so closely, in order to make of it the instrument of His graces to the world?

The human genealogy of Jesus ends with Mary, the Virgin of Nazareth, whom all generations declare blessed. From her, and through her from us, the Word asked a human nature, and Mary, in the power of the Holy Spirit, gave it to Him. That is why we shall always see her inseparable from Jesus and His mysteries. Wherever Jesus is found, we shall see her, He is her Son as much as He is the Son of God.

However, if Jesus everywhere remains the Son of Mary, especially in the mysteries of His childhood and hidden life is He revealed under this precise aspect. If Mary everywhere occupies a unique place, it is in these mysteries that her position as His Mother is most actively manifested outwardly and her divine Maternity shines forth most brightly. This incomparable dignity is the source of all the other privileges of the Virgin.

Mary's faith was perfect, and, filled with the light of the Holy Spirit, her soul understood the value of the offering that she was making to God. By His inspirations, the Holy Spirit put her soul in harmony with the inward dispositions of the Heart of her divine Son. This intense faith which was a source of love for the Mother of

---

[2] Matthew 1:16; Galatians 4:4.   [3] Romans 1:3.
[4] John 1:16.   [5] John 3:16.

God, was also a principle of joy. The Holy Spirit Himself teaches us this, by the mouth of Elizabeth, when He declares that the Virgin is blessed forever because of her faith.[6]

Those who do not know the Blessed Virgin, those who do not truly love the Mother of Jesus, run the risk of not profitable understanding the mysteries of Christ's humanity. Christ is the Son of Man as well as the Son of God; these two characters are essential to Him. If He is the Son of God by an eternal ineffable generation, He became the Son of Man by being born of Mary in time.

Let us contemplate this Virgin at the side of her Son; in return, she will obtain for us the power of entering more deeply into the comprehension of these mysteries to which she is so closely united.

In order that the exchange which God willed to contract with humanity should be possible, it was necessary that humanity should consent to it.

Let us transport ourselves to Nazareth. The fullness of time has come. God decreed, St. Paul tells us, to send His Son into the world in causing Him to be born of a woman. The angel Gabriel, God's messenger, brings to the young Jewish maiden the heavenly proposals. A sublime dialog takes place whereon hangs the deliverance of the human race.[7]

The angel first salutes the maiden declaring her, in the name of God, "full of grace." Indeed, not only is she sinless, no stain has tarnished her soul,—the Church has defined that she, alone among all creatures, has not been touched by original sin;—but moreover, because He has predestined her to be the Mother of His Son, the eternal Father has lavished His gifts upon her. She is full of grace, not of course as Christ is to be, for He is so by right and with the divine plenitude itself; Mary receives all in participation, but in a measure which cannot be estimated, and in correlation with her eminent dignity as Mother of God.

"Behold," says the angel, "Thou shalt conceive in thy womb and bring forth a Son, and thou shalt call His name Jesus . . . He shall be called the Son of the most high God . . . and He shall be king over the House of Jacob forever." "How shall this happen," asks Mary, "since I do not know man?" For she wishes to keep her

[6] Luke 1:45; 11:27.
[7] For a more thorough treatment of this idea in the writings of the Fathers, see: Dollen, *A Voice Said Ave!* (Boston: St. Paul editions).

virginity. " The Holy Spirit shall come upon thee and the power of the Most High shall overshadow thee; and therefore the Holy One to be born shall be called the Son of God." " Behold the handmaid of the Lord; be it done to me according to thy word."[8]

In this solemn moment, the exchange is concluded. When Mary pronounces her *Fiat,* all humanity says to God by her mouth, " Yes, O God, I consent, so be it! " And immediately, the Word is made flesh.[9] At this instant, the Word becomes incarnate by the operation of the Holy Spirit; the Blessed Virgin becomes the Ark of the New Covenant between God and man. Her own soul, guided by the Holy Spirit, comes into perfect conformity with the soul of her Son.

When the Church sings, in the Credo, the words that recall this mystery, " And was made flesh by the Holy Spirit, of the Virgin Mary: And was made man " she obliges her ministers to bend the knee in token of adoration. Let us, to, adore this Divine Word made man for us in the womb of a Virgin; let us adore Him with so much the more love, the more He humbles Himself in taking, as St. Paul says, " the form of a servant."[10] Let us adore Him in union with Mary, who, enlightened with the light of the Holy Spirit, bows down before her Creator become her Son. Let us adore Him with the angels marvelling at this infinite condescension towards humanity.

Let us next salute Our Lady, and thank her for having given Jesus to us. It is to her consent that we owe Him.[11] Let us add our congratulations. Consider how the Holy Spirit by the mouth of Elizabeth, saluted her almost on the day of the Incarnation: " Blessed art thou among women and blessed is the the fruit of thy womb! . . . And blessed is she who has believed, because the things promised her by the Lord shall be accomplished."[12] Blessed, for this faith in God's word made the Virgin the Mother of Christ. What simple creature has ever received like praises from the infinite Being?

Mary refers to the Lord the glory of the marvels wrought in her. She sings within her heart a canticle full of love and gratitude. With her cousin Elizabeth, she lets the innermost feelings of her heart overflow; she sings the *Magnificat* which, throughout the centuries, her children will repeat after her in praise of God for having chosen her out of all women. Her heart is so in tune with the Holy Spirit that she can sing forth: " My soul magnifies the Lord and my spirit

---

[8] Luke 1:28-38.   [9] John 1:14.   [10] Philippians 2:7.
[11] Collect for the office of the Circumcision.   [12] Luke 1:41-45.

rejoices in God my Saviour, because he has regarded the lowliness of his handmaid . . . because he who is mighty has done great things for me."[13]

Mary was at Bethlehem for the enrollment ordered by Caesar when, says St. Luke, " the days for her to be delivered were fulfilled. And she brought forth her firstborn son and wrapped him in swaddling clothes and laid him in a manger, because there was no room for them in the inn."[14] Who is this Child? He is Mary's Son, since He has just been born of her.

But she saw in this Child, a child like other children, the Very Son of God. Mary's soul was full of immense faith, which went very far beyond the faith of all the just of the Old Testament. Therefore, in her Son, she saw her God.

This faith translated itself outwardly in an act of adoration. As soon as she looked upon Jesus, the Maiden-Mother adored Him with an intensity that we cannot conceive.

To this intense faith, this deep adoration, were added the transports of an incommensurable love, a love both human and supernatural. The workings of the Holy Spirit found full play with in her soul as she contemplated the God-Man.

God is love, and so that we may have some idea of this love, He gives a share of it to mothers. The heart of a mother, with her unwearying tenderness, the constancy of her solicitude, the inexhaustible delicacy of her affection is a truly divine creation, although God has placed in her only a spark of His love for us. Yet, however imperfectly a mother's heart reflects the divine love towards us, God gives us our mothers to take His place in some manner with us. He places them at our side, from our cradles, to guide us, to guard us, especially in our earliest years when we have so much need of tenderness.

Imagine, then, with what predilection the Holy Trinity fashioned the immaculate heart of the Blessed Virgin, chosen to be the Mother of the Incarnate Word. God delighted in pouring forth love in her heart, in forming it expressly to love a God-Man.

In Mary's heart were perfectly harmonized the adoration of a creature towards her God, and the love of a mother for her only Son.

The supernatural love of Our Lady is not less wonderful. As you know, a soul's love for God is measured by its degree of grace. What

[13] Luke 1:46, 49.   [14] Luke 2:6-7.

is it that, in us, hinders the development of grace and love? Our
sins, our deliberate faults, our voluntary infidelities, our attachments
to creatures. Each deliberate fault narrows the heart, and strengthens
egotism. But Our Lady's soul is of perfect purity; unstained by sin,
untouched by any shadow of a fault, she is full of grace. Far from
encountering in her any obstacle to the unfolding of grace, the Holy
Spirit ever found her heart wonderfully docile to His inspirations,
and therefore full of love.

What must have been the joy of the soul of Jesus to feel Himself
loved to such an extent by His mother!

After the incomprehensible joy arising from the Beatific Vision and
from the look of infinite complacency wherewith the heavenly Father
contemplated Him, nothing can have rejoiced Him so much as the
love of His Mother. He found in it a more abundant compensation
for the indifference of those who would not receive Him. He found
in the heart of this young Virgin a fire of undying love that He
Himself further enkindled by His divine glances and the inward
grace of His Spirit.

Jesus gave Himself to Mary in such an ineffable manner, and
Mary corresponded so fully that after the union of the Divine
Persons in the Trinity, and the hypostatic union of the Incarnation,
we cannot conceive one greater nor deeper.

Moreover, it is through the Incarnation itself that the humanity of
Jesus was "consecrated", "anointed."[15] Not with an outward
anointing, as is done for simple creatures, but with an entirely
spiritual unction. By the action of the Holy Spirit, whom the liturgy
calls a "spiritual unction"[16] the Divinity is poured out upon the
human nature of Jesus like an "oil of gladness"[17] This unction is so
penetrating, the humanity is so closely consecrated to God, that no
closer consecration could be possible, for this human nature has
become the very humanity of a God, of the Son of God. Consider,
then, the dignity of Mary since, through the operations of the Holy
Spirit in her, she is rightfully given the title "Mother of the Incarnate Word."

And, at the moment of the Incarnation, whereby the first Priest of
the New Alliance was consecrated, a cry resounded in Heaven, "Thou
art a priest forever . . ."[18] St. Paul, whose gaze pierced so many

---

[15] St. Augustine, *De Trinitate*, 15:27.   [16] Hymn *Veni Creator*.
[17] Psalm 44:8.   [18] Psalm 109:4.

mysteries, likewise reveals this one to us. Listen to what he says. "And no man takes the honour to himself; he takes it who was called by God, as Aaron was. So also Christ did not glorify himself with the high priesthood, but he who spoke of him, 'Thou art my Son, I this day have begotten Thee.' As he says also in another place, 'Thou art a priest forever, according to the order of Melchisedech.'"[19]

Christ's priesthood is a necessary and immediate consequence of the Incarnation which unites God and man. Truly, this work of the Holy Spirit, bringing Christ into the world through Mary, merits for her the title "Mother of the Eternal Priest," and, indeed, mother of all priests.

Let us draw near to Mary with a humble but entire confidence. If her Son is the Saviour of the world, she enters too deeply into His mission not to share the love that He bears to sinners. "O Mother of our Redeemer," let us sing with the Church, "thou didst bear Thy Creator whilst remaining a Virgin, succour this fallen race which thy Son came to save in taking a human nature."[20] Have pity upon the sinners whom thy Son came to redeem. For, O Mary, it was to redeem us that He vouchsafed to descend from the eternal splendours into your virginal bosom.

[19] Hebrews 5:4-6.
[20] Hymn *Alma Redemptoris Mater*.

Bibliography

WORKS BY ABBOT MARMION

Christ in His Mysteries. Sands & Co. and B. Herder
Christ the ideal of the Monk. Sands & Co. and B. Herder
Christ the ideal of the Priest. Sands & Co. and B. Herder
Christ the Life of the Soul. Sands & Co. and B. Herder
Consecration a la Sainte Trinite. Editions de Maredsous
English Letters of Dom Columba Marmion. Helicon
Les Mysteres du Rosaire. Editions de Maredsous
Sponsa Verbi. Sands & Co. and B. Herder
Union with God. Sands & Co. and B. Herder
Way of the Cross. Sands & Co. and B. Herder
Words of Life on the Margin of the Missal. Sands & Co. and B. Herder

BOOKS ABOUT ABBOT MARMION AND HIS TEACHING

Marmion, Columba. *More About Dom Marmion.* B. Herder
Philipon, Marie Michel. *Spiritual doctrine of Sister Elizabeth of the Trinity.* Newman
Thibaut, Raymond. *Abbot Columba Marmion.* Sands & Co. and B. Herder

BOOKS ON THE HOLY SPIRIT

Biskiepek, Aloysius. *Come Creator Spirit.* Techny, III, Mission Press, 1949
Blunt, Hugh. *Life with the Holy Ghost.* Milwaukee, Bruce, 1943
Buddy, Charles Francis. *Send forth Thy Spirit.* 4th ed., rev. and enlarged. Boston, St. Paul Editions, 1959
Dooley, Lester M. *Discourses on the Holy Ghost.* N.Y., Joseph F. Wagner, 1942

Dooley, Lester M. *Further Discourses on the Holy Ghost*. N.Y., Frederick Pustet Co., Inc., 1945

Farrell, Walter. *Companion to the Summa*. N.Y., Sheed and Ward, 1945. (Note particularly volume 2, chapter 12.)

Froget, Barthelemy. *Indwelling of the Holy Spirit*. N.Y., Paulist Press, 1921

Gihr, Nicholas. *The Veni Sancte Spiritus*. Techny, III, Mission Press (?), 1947

Henry, A. M. *The Holy Spirit*. N.Y., Hawthorn Books, 1960

Hilary of Poitiers, St. *The Trinity*. N.Y., Fathers of the Church, Inc., 1954

Jarrett, Bede. *The abiding presence of the Holy Spirit*. London, Burns, Oates and Washbourne, 1935

Kelly, Bernard. *The seven gifts of the Holy Ghost*. N.Y., Sheed and Ward, 1941

Leen, Edward. *The Holy Ghost and His work in souls*. N.Y., Sheed and Ward, 1940

Lefebvre, Gaspar. *The Spirit of worship*. N.Y., Hawthorn Books, 1959

McAstocker, David P. *The Consoler*. Milwaukee, Bruce, 1938

McMahon, John T. *The Gift of God: Come Holy Spirit*. Westminster, Md., Newman Press, 1958

Manning, Henry Edward. *The internal mission of the Holy Ghost*. N.Y., P. J. Kenedy, 1900

Manning, Henry Edward. *The temporal mission of the Holy Ghost*. N.Y., P. J. Kenedy, 1896

Martinez, Luis Maria. *The Sanctifier*. Paterson, N.J., St. Anthony Guild Press, 1957

Sheen, Fulton J. *The divine romance*. Garden City, N.Y., Garden City Publishing Co., 1930

Stadelman, William. *Glories of the Holy Ghost*. Techny, III, Mission Press, 1919

Vonier, Anscar. *The Spirit and the Bride*. London, Burns, Oates and Washbourne, 1935

Woollen, C. J. *The twelve fruits*. N.Y., J. F. Wagner, 1950

Zardetti, Otto. *Special devotion to the Holy Ghost*. Milwaukee, Hoffman Brothers, 1888

Index

Adam, 49, 101-102
Advocate, 19, 31, 32, 38, 39, 45, 96
Angels, 20, 25, 27, 69, 115-116
Appropriation, 22-23, 52
Ascension, 31, 33, 43, 73, 76, 96
Augustine, St., 34, 40-41, 49, 93, 97

Baptism, 18, 37, 40, 41, chap. 12, 68, 78, 84, 97, 99, 102, 105, 108-109, 111, 112
Benedict, St., 79-80, 85-86
Bossuet, 23
Bruyere, Madame Cecile, 83

Cana, 81
Catherine of Siena, St., 82
Cenacle, 34, 42
Children of God, see Grace of Adoption
Church, 7, 11, 32, 33, chap. 9, 69 seq., chap. 11, 67, 70, 73, 82, 96, 115, 116, 119
Comforter, 43
Conditions for prayer, chap. 21, 92-93, 97, 101
Confirmation, 40, 68, 99, 102, 108-109, 111, 113
Consoler, 32, 38-39, 67
Council of Orange, 90
Council of Trent, 50
Counsel (gift), 57, 65, chap. 16, 99
Creed, 21, 27, 46, 73, 116

Distinction of persons, see Procession of Persons
Divine Office, 82, 83, 110
Doyle, Fr. William, 110

Eve, 102
Extreme Unction, 40

Fabre, Fr. Peter, 110
Faith, 34, 45, 55, 62, 63, 70, 72, 77-78, 91, 96, 97, 102, 104, 110, 113, 114, 116-117
Fear of the Lord (gift), 59-60, chap. 15, 77, 99
Fortitude (gift), 37, 58, chap. 15, 99

Francis Borgia, St., 86
Francis de Sales, St., 87
Fruits of the Holy Spirit, 60-61

Gifts of the Holy Spirit, 37, 41, 42, 47-48, 53-56, chap. 14, 77-78, 98, 101, 106, 107, 113. See also individual gifts
Grace of Adoption, 8, 11, 25, 44-45, chap. 12, 52, 71, 74, 75, 84, 95, 96, 99, 101, 102-104, 112, 114

Holiness, 20, 22, 23, 24, 25, 36, 42, 44, 47, 52, 78, 100, 103
High Priest (Christ), 38, 39, 43, 62, 68, 69, 70, 71, 101, 119
Holy Communion, 44, 45, 67, 68, 70, 113
Holy Orders, 40, 68, 69, 108-109, 112
Hypostatic Union, 27, 111, 118

Ignatius Loyola, St., 86
Illuminative Way, 92, 94-95, 97-98
Incarnation, 20, 26, 31, 71, 75, 103, 111, 113, 116, 118
Indwelling of the Holy Spirit, 12, 47, chap. 13, 99, 102, 108, 112
Infallibility, 43
Isaiah, 28-29, 80

John XXIII, Pope, 7
John Baptist, St., 29
John Chrysostom, St., 110
John the Evangelist, St., 34, 91, 95, 97

Knowledge (gift), 55, 59, chap. 16, 77, 99

Last Supper, 12, 18, 26
Leo XIII, Pope, 13, 22, 41
Leo, St., 34
Liturgy, 40, 47, 54, 61, 63, 65, 67, chap. 19, 83-84, 96, 106, 118
Love, 15, 16-17, 22, 26, 27, 33, 36-37, 43, 44, 47, 52-53, 61-62, 68, 70, 72, 78, 79, 89, 97, 99, 104, 107, 110, 112, 114-115, 117-118
Luke, St., 76, 117

Magdalen, 91, 104

Magnificat, the, 116
Mary, Blessed Virgin, 20, 27, 28, 68, 69, 71, 74, 84, 90-91, 93, 111, chap. 31
Matrimony, 40
Mass, Holy, 61 seq., 63, 65, 66 seq., 69
Methods of Prayer, 87-88
Michael, St., 102
Mortal sin, 80, 100
Mystical Body, 7, 8, 39, 72

Nature, 14-15, 103
New Pentecost, 7, 33, chap. 10, 110
Nicodemus, 49

" Our Father ", 76, 78

Paraclete, 34, 45, 103
Passion of Christ, 33, 38, 46, 61, 69
Paul, St., 11, 16, 25, 30, 33, 38, 40, 41, 44, 49, 50, 52, 53, 64, 68, 73, 74, 80, 81, 84, 90, 95, 100, 102, 108, 112, 115, 116
Penance, 40
Pentecost, 7, 32, 33, chap. 8, 39, 44, 46, 106. See also New Pentecost
Peter, St., 32, 37-38, 46, 49
Piety (gift), 59, chap. 15, 77, 99-100
Pontiff, see: High Priest (Christ)
Prayer, chap. 20, 79, 85, 89, 92, 97, 100, chap. 27, 104, 109, 111, 113
Preparation for prayer, see Conditions for prayer
Priests, 40, 62, 65, chap. 18
Procession of Persons, chap. 3, 20-22, 26, 33, 34-35, 46-47, 53, 106, 113

Psalms, 82, 110
Purgative Way, 92

Resurrection, 38, 71

Sacraments, see individual sacraments
Samaritan Woman, the, 75
Sanctification, 12, 22, 45, 47, 54, 56, 73, 103
Sanctifier, 67
Sanctifying grace, 27-28, 44, 53, 88 seq., 90, 103, 106
Simeon, 91
Sons of God, see Grace of Adoption

Teresa, St., 77, 81, 86, 95-96
Thomas, Apostle, St., 34
Thomas Aquinas, St., 22, 24, 26, 27, 41, 55, 64, 90, 92
Trinity, Most Holy, chap. 2, 17, 19-20, 22, 23, 50-51, 68, 99, 103, 118

Understanding (gift), 55, 57, chap. 16, 77, 98, 99
Unitive Way, 92, 98
Unity of God, 15

Virtues, 47-48, 53, 55, 113

Wisdom (gift), 56, chap. 17, 78, 98, 99
Word, the, 14, 22, 23, 27-28, 30, 33, 35, 61, 68, 71, 75, 76, 83, 96, 106, 111, 116, 117

Zacharias, 77